HISTORY

IN

100

NUMBERS

METRO BOOKS
New York

An Imprint of Sterling Publishing Co., Inc.
1166 Avenue of the Americas
New York, NY 10036

METRO BOOKS and the distinctive Metro Books logo
are trademarks of Sterling Publishing Co., Inc.

© 2016 by Quid Publishing

ISBN 978-1-4351-5799-6

For information about custom editions, special sales, and
premium and corporate purchases, please contact
Sterling Special Sales at 800-805-5489
or specialsales@sterlingpublishing.com.

Manufactured in China

2 4 6 8 10 9 7 5 3 1

www.sterlingpublishing.com

Design and illustration by Simon Daley

Conceived, designed, and produced by
Quid Publishing
Part of The Quarto Group
Level 4 Sheridan House
114 Western Road
Hove BN3 1DD
England

www.quidpublishing.com

HISTORY

IN

100

NUMBERS

Numerical Snapshots
of the Last 2,000 Years

JOEL LEVY

METRO BOOKS
New York

Table of contents

Introduction

Even when looking at only the Common Era, as this book does, it would be impossible to give a comprehensive coverage of the whole history of the last 2,000 years in just 100 numbers, so this book doesn't. Instead, it tries to discuss some of the most famous numbers in history, from the Hundred Years' War to 9/11, and also to demonstrate the fresh and powerful historical perspective that numbers can give.

Numbers can make the general, specific; they can sharpen the fuzzy outlines of history, adding precision to vague propositions. A frequent criticism of quantitative history is that it fails to capture the human element of history; that mere numbers cannot reflect individual experience. But precisely because of this, a numerical approach to history can actually rescue much more of the historical experience of the "common people," democratizing history. Numbers are particularly important in the study of groups, a vital counterbalance to the traditional focus of history on individuals. Quantitative history makes it possible to get away from the "great men" account of history, making accessible broader trends and movements, giving some sort of voice—often the only one possible—to the unrecorded ordinary people, their concerns and pursuits.

This is not to claim some sort of historical "purity" for numbers. In a field of slippery subjectivity, seemingly composed of opinion and interpretation, where narratives are often suspect for their agendas and assumptions, numbers might seem to offer some hope of objectivity. Surely numbers are "hard facts"; numbers don't lie? Of course this is wishful thinking. Who has done the counting? What did they choose to count and why? History is a social science, but it frequently struggles with the science bit.

"The problem for the historian," write Conal Furay and Michael J. Salevouris in *The Methods and Skills of History* (see Further reading, pp. 170–171), "is that numbers, like other forms of evidence, do not speak for themselves." I'm not sure I entirely agree; some numbers feel as though they can tell a whole story with a few digits. For instance, did you know that between 1619 and 1865, African-American slaves provided 222,505,049 hours of forced labor? Or that the Gettysburg Address lasted just two minutes? That 191 people were killed trying to cross the Berlin Wall, or that about 1000 sheep were skinned to make the Domesday Book? That poor Irish farmers in the 1840s ate up to 15 lb (7 kg) of potatoes a day, or that a quarter of the world's population took the day off for the coronation of Elizabeth II? That you could buy eight pigs, four oxen, 12 sheep, 12 tons (11 tonnes) of wheat, 48 tons (44 tonnes) of rye, two hogsheads of wine, four barrels of beer, two tons (1.8 tonnes) of butter, 1,000 lb (454 kg) of cheese, a silver drinking cup, and possibly even a ship for the price of a single tulip bulb in Holland in 1637? These and many other numbers in this book will entertain and inform you... you can count on it.

O

The year decreed by Khmer Rouge as the start of their new era

In 1975 an extreme Communist revolutionary movement called the Khmer Rouge took power in the Southeast Asian nation of Cambodia. Under their leader Pol Pot, they renamed the country Democratic Kampuchea, and declared that it was Year Zero. Society and culture would be reset to zero as the Khmer Rouge attempted to introduce a demented agrarian idyll. "We wish to do away with all vestiges of the past..." said Pol Pot, "There is no money, no commerce... There are no schools, faculties, or universities... The countryside should be the focus of attention of our revolution...." In the words of the journalist John Pilger, who did much to expose the horrors of the Khmer Rouge: "Year Zero was the dawn of an age in which, in extremis, there would be no families, no sentiment, no expression of love or grief, no medicines, no hospitals, no schools, no books, no learning, no vacations, no music: only work and death."

Achieving this fantasy required the most horrific genocide since Nazism and Stalinism: "We will burn the old grass and new will grow," said the Khmer Rouge. Hundreds of thousands were murdered by fanatical young cadres, their absence of regard for human life summed up by the Khmer Rouge dictum: "To keep you is no benefit, to destroy you is no loss." Many more died from disease, starvation, and exhaustion.

In the space of little more than three years an estimated 1.7 million people died (possibly more), out of a pregenocide population of about 7 million.

▲ Pol Pot, the Khmer Rouge leader. Born Saloth Sar in 1925, he studied in Paris before returning to lead a Communist insurrection in Cambodia and presiding over a horrific dystopia.

2/3

The proportion of the Great Wall of China remaining

While the Great Wall of China cannot, contrary to popular myth, be seen from space with the unaided human eye, it is the longest architectural structure ever built by humans. In fact it is not one but several walls, built over the course of nearly 2,000 years. Before the unification of China, regional states, particularly those in the north, built independent stretches of wall. These were joined to give a single, great wall by the first Qin emperor, Shihuangdi, who unified China in 221 BCE, at least according to the traditional version of the Wall's history. By the Han period (206 BCE–220 CE) the total length of the wall was over 10,000 *li* (a Chinese unit of measurement equating to about 0.3 miles [0.5 km], making the wall around 3,000 miles [5,000 km] long), and so it became known as the *Wanli Changcheng*, the "Ten-thousand-li-long Wall."

The gates of heaven

The Great Wall as it is known today is almost entirely the work of the Ming Dynasty (1368–1644), who are said to have constructed over 5,500 miles (8,800 km) of wall, while the total length of the walls constructed throughout Chinese history is said to be up to 13,171 miles (21,196 km). The length of the route covered by the Wall, however, is much less; it stretches across around 3,900 miles (6,300 km), running from the Jiayuguan Pass of Gansu Province in the west to the Shanhaiguan Pass of Hebei Province

▼ The best preserved and most scenic stretch of the wall is a modern-era restoration of a Ming Dynasty structure.

in the east, where its terminus is marked by a monument called the "first door under heaven." The Ming Wall stands up to 26 feet (8 m) high, averaging 15–30 feet (4.7–9.1 m) in thickness at the base and sloping to 12 feet (3.7 m) thick at the top. It was fortified by 25,000 towers and 15,000 outposts, although long stretches, especially in the west, consist only of high mounds and ditches.

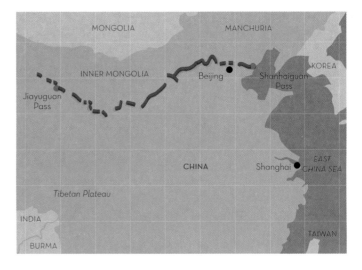

▲ The remaining stretches of the Great Wall, constituting about two-thirds of the extent present during the Ming Dynasty.

The supposed purpose of the Wall was to prevent incursions from the horse-riding, nomadic, "barbarian" peoples of the northern steppes. Perhaps because it never proved effective at this, the Wall was abandoned by the Qing (Manchu) Dynasty (1644–1912) and left to fall into disrepair. Only in the late 20th century was it conserved and rebuilt in places as a tourist attraction and national icon.

Tears and tall tales

The traditional account of the Great Wall tells of the extraordinary labors demanded by the despotic First Emperor, Shihuangdi, who pressed a significant proportion of the Chinese population into working on the project. In the harsh and dangerous conditions of the giant building site, tens of thousands died and were interred in the wall. According to the work of historian Arthur Waldron, however, much of this story is a myth; he contends that evidence for the pre-Ming Wall is scant and that the Great Wall only came into being under the Ming.

1

Female pope

The legend of Pope Joan claims that in 853 a woman disguised as a man was elected Pope, only to be unmasked—with fatal consequences—when she gave birth while processing through the streets of Rome. According to various versions of this tall tale, a young woman from either England or Germany was taken to Athens by her lover and there gained an education, proving to be a brilliant scholar and theologian. Adopting the guise of Johannes Anglicus, or perhaps John of Mainz, she started lecturing in Rome, gaining a reputation for learning and probity that saw her elected first cardinal, and then, following the demise of Leo IV, Pope.

For two years she concealed her secret, but fell pregnant by the one man who knew the truth, leading to her unfortunate obstetric unmasking in 855. The good people of Rome offered their own brand of postnatal care, dragging her by her ankles behind a horse through the streets of Rome, while pelting her with stones. According to the legend, the transvestite theocrat so shook the authorities that they henceforth added a "genital inspection" element to papal inaugurations, while papal processions have since avoided the street where Joan gave birth.

Alas, this entertaining tale is almost universally accepted as a fiction. Pope Leo IV actually died in 855 and was succeeded without interruption by Benedict III. There are no contemporary mentions of Pope Joan. Papal processions avoid the off-limits alley because it is too narrow, and new popes emphatically do not undergo a gender test.

▼ The legend of Pope Joan, in which the 9th-century female impostor is given away in dramatic fashion by giving birth in the midst of a procession.

1

Giant leap for mankind

On July 20th, 1969, at 10:56 pm, Eastern Daylight Time, Neil Armstrong put his left foot on the surface of the moon and broadcast his famous comment: "That's one small step for a man, one giant leap for mankind." Thanks to his central Ohio accent, however, most of the listening millions back on Earth thought he'd missed out the "a" (see box).

The Space Race

Armstrong's historic step was the culmination of one of the greatest ever feats of science, technology, and engineering: the Apollo lunar-landing program. The Apollo program was phase three of an ambitious plan conceived at the outset of the Space Race, the Cold War rivalry between the USA and the Soviets for mastery of space. In the years after World War II, America was generally considered to have neglected missile technology, and in 1957 Americans were horrified when the Russians successfully launched *Sputnik*, the first artificial satellite, into orbit aboard a modified intercontinental ballistic missile.

The Soviets followed this up by launching into orbit the first animal, Laika the dog; the first space probe to reach the moon, with *Luna 2* in 1959; and the first man in space, with Yuri Gagarin in April 1961. The Americans, scrambling to catch up, created the National Aeronautics and Space Administration (NASA) in 1958, and even changed their public school curriculum to boost the

▲ Apollo 11 blasts off on its historic mission to the moon, July 16th, 1969.

The case of the missing "A"

One of the great legends about the moon landing is that Armstrong fluffed his historic line, forgetting the indefinite article that would have protected his statement from tautology. In fact acoustic studies have shown that, although it was indistinguishable to most listeners in the poor-quality transmission from the moon, Armstrong did say "one small step for a man." However, his central Ohio accent meant that "if the word 'a' was spoken, it was very short and was fully blended acoustically with the preceding word," according to Laura Dilley, assistant professor of communicative sciences and disorders at Michigan State University. So what sounds like "frrr(uh)" is actually Armstrong's way of saying "for a."

mathematics and science education that would be needed to produce engineers and scientists for the space program.

Mercury, Gemini, and Apollo

The first phase in what would become the lunar-landing program was Project Mercury, which succeeded in putting an American in space for the first time on May 5th, 1961, when Alan Shepard was launched on a 15-minute sub-orbital flight. Later that month President John F. Kennedy set the famous goal of going to the moon by the end of the decade, and NASA began to grow exponentially. Between 1961 and 1964 its budget increased almost fivefold, and it would eventually employ 34,000 people directly, with another 375,000 personnel from industry and academia working on contract.

The second phase in the program was Project Gemini, with multiple missions in Earth orbit to test and develop the equipment and techniques that would be needed for the moon shot. In 1968 the first Apollo mission was launched, and in December of that year *Apollo 8* went all the way to the moon, around it, and back to Earth. At 9:32 am on July 16th, 1969, *Apollo 11* took off from Cape Kennedy in Florida. On board were Commander Neil A. Armstrong, Command Module Pilot Michael Collins, and Lunar

Module Pilot Edwin E. (Buzz) Aldrin, Jr. All three were 39 years old, weighed 165 lb (75 kg), and stood just under 6 feet (1.8 m) tall.

Godspeed

An estimated 1 million people watched the launch in person, including half of the U.S. Congress and over 3,000 reporters from 56 countries. As the massive, 363 foot (111 m) tall rocket lifted off with 7.6 million pounds (34.5 million newtons) of thrust (equivalent to the power output of 85 Hoover Dams), Launch Control wished the astronauts "Good luck and Godspeed." Just over 3 hours later, as the spacecraft hurtled toward the moon at around 24,000 mph (38,600 km/h), the astronauts had to disassemble and then reassemble it in a complex maneuver, in which the command module Columbia, the main part of the spacecraft, was separated from the lunar-landing module Eagle, turned around, and docked head-to-head with it.

After three days' travel, *Apollo 11* reached the moon and went into lunar orbit. At 1:46 pm on July 20th the lunar-landing craft, carrying Armstrong and Aldrin, separated from the command module. Collins was left to orbit the moon alone for more than a day, prompting Mission Control to muse that "Not since Adam has any human known such solitude as Mike Collins is experiencing during this 47 minutes of each lunar revolution when he's behind the moon with no one to talk to except his tape recorder aboard Columbia." Just after 4 pm, as the lander neared the lunar surface, Armstrong took manual command of the controls, piloting away from the rocky crater to which they had been heading. Monitors recording his heartbeat showed that it had doubled; Aldrin's voice, giving altitude and attitude readings, remained

Moon's orbit

Return journey

Launch

Command module splashdown and recovery

Outward journey

Lunar module launch

Lunar module descent

▲ The Apollo 11 mission called for a series of perfectly choreographed maneuvers to transition between Earth and lunar orbits.

calm: "400 feet, down at nine... Got the shadow out there... 75 feet, things looking good... Picking up some dust... 30 feet, 2 ½ down... Four forward. Four forward, drifting to the right a little... Contact light. Okay, engine stop." At 4:18 pm the lander came to rest on the surface of the moon. "The Eagle has landed," Armstrong radioed to Mission Control.

Down the ladder

At 10:39 pm Armstrong opened the hatch of the lunar lander and squeezed out. The low lunar gravity meant that his bulky suit and portable life support unit, which weighed 84 lb (38 kg) back on Earth, were just over 14 lb (6 kg) on the moon. On the second rung of the ladder Armstrong pulled a ring to switch on a television camera that would broadcast his descent and first step. On the ninth and last rung, he paused to report "I'm at the foot of the ladder... the surface appears to be very, very finegrained, as you get close to it, it's almost like a powder." Then he placed his foot on the surface of another world.

After a day spent deploying a number of science experiments and an American flag, taking many pictures, and taking a phone call from President Richard Nixon, Aldrin and Armstrong clambered back into the Eagle for a nap. At 1:54 pm on July 21st the lunar-ascent module lifted off from the moon to rendezvous with Collins on board *Columbia*. Together the three astronauts set off back to Earth, splashing down in the Pacific at 12:51 pm on July 24th. Their spacecraft had traveled 1.1 million miles (1.76 million km), and their mission of 195 hours, 18 minutes, and 35 seconds (just over eight days) had been completed without a hitch.

▲ (Top) The three Apollo 11 astronauts, from right to left: Armstrong, Collins, and Aldrin. (Above) Buzz Aldrin's footprints, visible at the bottom of the photo, are still there.

1

Year as decreed by the French Revolutionary Calendar

The Revolutionary Calendar of the French Republic began with the Year One, corresponding to September 22nd, 1792– September 21st, 1793, in the rest of Europe. In fact there never was a Year One, and the Revolutionary Calendar itself never made it past Year Fourteen.

Time for a change

In the fall of 1793 the Revolutionary Convention decreed that henceforth France would no longer follow the Gregorian calendar used in the rest of the Western world. Instead a new calendar was to be introduced, marking a radical break with the past. This new calendar would have new days, new months, and new years, and was decreed to have started on September 22nd, 1792, the day on which the French Republic had been founded, which had also been the fall equinox. Since the new calendar was not adopted until after September 22nd, 1793, there never was a Year One, although the date was applied retrospectively. Instead the new calendar started in Year Two.

The new calendar was part of the Revolutionary project to sweep away the old world, and in particular instruments associated with the aristocracy and the Church. Accordingly a committee was established to draw up a new, purely secular calendar. Deciding when it should start was one topic of debate. Some proposed Bastille Day (July 14th, 1789), others the start of the revolutionary year (i.e. January 1st, 1789). French astronomer Jérôme Lalande pointed out that the founding of the Republic had fallen on the fall equinox of 1792, and his friend, mathematician turned politician Gilbert Romme, waxed lyrical in support of the proposal to start the new calendar on this date: "Thus, the sun illuminated both poles simultaneously, and in succession the entire globe, on the same day that, for the first time, in all its purity, the flame of liberty, which must one day illuminate all mankind, shone on the French nation."

The new calendar was constructed on rational lines, with the 365 days of the year divided into 12 months of 30 days each, followed by five additional holidays (six in a leap year). There would be no more Sundays, and no more religious holidays: "No creation of the republic," declared Lalande, "will do more to break the hold of the priests over their superstitious dupes."

Nippy, Drippy, and Slippy

The months, named by the poet Philippe Fabre d'Églantine in rhyming triplets, were Vendémiaire ("wine harvest" or "vintage"), Brumaire ("mist"), and Frimaire ("frost"), in the fall; Nivôse ("snow"), Pluviôse ("rain"), and Ventôse ("wind"), in winter; Germinal ("seedtime"), Floréal ("blossom"), and Prairial ("meadow"), in spring; and Messidor ("harvest"), Thermidor ("heat"), and Fructidor ("fruits") in summer. The British irreverently rechristened them Nippy, Drippy, Slippy, Freezy, Sneezy, Wheezy, Showery, Flowery, Bowery, Wheaty, Heaty, and Sweety.

The Revolutionary or Republican Calendar was abandoned by Napoleon in an attempt to get the Catholic Church on his side, and France reverted to the Gregorian calendar on January 1st, 1806.

▼ Allegory of the month Germinal.

GERMINAL.

3

Roman legions lost in the Teutoburg Forest

In the year 9 CE, the Roman army suffered one of the greatest disasters in its history when three entire legions were wiped out in an ambush by Germans, deep in the Teutoburg Forest. The defeat had profound and lasting consequences for the Roman empire and the course of European history.

Around the start of the Common Era, the Roman empire under Augustus was working to consolidate conquests in Germania, along the Rhine. The process of Romanizing Germanic tribes was underway, with German princes serving in the Roman military and German tribes starting to be urbanized. Augustus' heir, Tiberius, had extended Roman control across the Rhine as far as the Elbe, but in 7 CE he was recalled and replaced by Publius Quinctilius Varus. One of Varus' closest native allies was a German prince known to the Romans as Arminius (and to Germans as Herman). What Varus did not know was that Arminius was plotting a rebellion, and laying a terrible trap for the Romans.

In late summer of 9 CE, Arminius arranged reports of trouble in what is now Lower Saxony. Varus mobilized three legions—the XVII, XVIII, and XIX—and marched them deep into the marshy forest, and directly into a carefully laid trap. Strung out along the difficult forest track, the Romans were harassed and picked off by German raiders, and eventually ambushed. "Never was there slaughter more cruel than took place there in the marshes and woods, never were more intolerable insults inflicted by barbarians," recorded the Roman historian Florus in his *Epitome*.

▲ According to Roman historian Suetonius, when Augustus (pictured) heard the news, "He was so greatly affected that for several months in succession he cut neither his beard nor his hair, and sometimes he could dash his head against a door, crying 'Quinctilius Varus, give me back my legions!'"

3

The Three Kingdoms
period of Chinese history

The Three Kingdoms period of Chinese history is said to date from 220-265 (or 280; see box, page 22), from the end of the Han Dynasty to the start of the short-lived Jin Dynasty. Although it was a bloody and chaotic period that led to a dramatic fall in population and prosperity, its romantic image looms large in Chinese cultural imagination, in similar fashion to the way that Europeans romanticize the medieval period as the "Age of Chivalry."

The Eastern Han empire had ruled China since 25 CE, but by the end of the 2nd century it was falling apart. Corrupt and ineffective rulers had ceded control to court eunuchs, while natural disasters and famines helped convince the population that the Han had lost legitimacy (otherwise known as "the Mandate of Heaven").

Rebellions and intrigues drove the last Han emperor, Xian, to take refuge with his most powerful general, Cao Cao, in 195. Cao Cao now assumed effective control of the throne, but his authority was confined to the region to the north of the Yangtze River, while below the Yangtze the land was divided into two

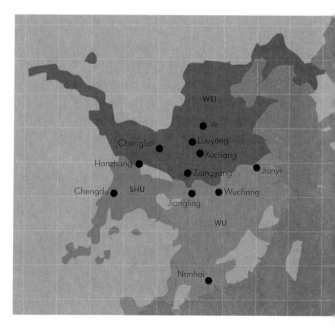

▼ The Three Kingdoms of 3rd-century China, a time of war and chaos heavily romanticized by later writers.

End of an era

The Three Kingdoms period ended when Wei finally conquered the kingdoms to the south. Power politics in Wei had seen the rise of the Sima clan, under leading general Sima Yan, although the Cao clan nominally retained the throne. In 263 a Wei army invaded and conquered Shu, and in 265 Sima Yan forced the last Cao king to abdicate in his favor, and established the Jin (or Tsin) Dynasty. In some datings this marks the end of the Three Kingdoms period, but an alternative end date is 280, when the Jin finally subjugated Wu after a ten-year program of naval construction and invasion planning. In 279 a fleet of ships ferried the Jin army across the Yangtze, and in 280 Sun Hao, king of Wu, surrendered. The Jin now ruled all of China, but their hold on the empire would be short-lived and China would soon relapse into chaos.

kingdoms, Shu in the southwest, under Liu Bei, and Wu in the southeast, under Sun Quan.

Red Cliffs

Marshaling his forces, Cao Cao marched south, but an alliance between Shu and Wu armies defeated him at the Battle of Red Cliffs in 208. The de facto division of China into three kingdoms was now established, although the Han Dynasty only officially ended in 220 when Cao Cao's son and heir, Cao Pi, forced Xian to abdicate in his favor. Wei in the north was the most populous and powerful kingdom, but Shu and Wu built their strength through conquest and trade with each other (helped by grand canal projects) and with kingdoms to the south. In Wu, trade and shipping brought wealth and development, with a new capital city at Jianye (now called Nanjing) that would later become the capital of all China.

3

Kingdoms of ancient Korea

The Three Kingdoms of ancient Korea (57 BCE–668 CE), mark the emergence of Korea into recorded history. For seven centuries Korea was divided into three major states, Koguryo in the north, Paekche in the southwest, and Silla in the southeast. These kingdoms arose from tribal cultures, where peasants supported a militaristic elite who lived in walled cities, controlling the important metallurgical industry.

The primary influence on these states was the advanced Chinese civilization to the north, and Koguryo was the first to emerge in reaction to a Chinese colony established by the Han. When the Han Dynasty collapsed (see page 21), the power vacuum in the region left space for the development of other powerful small states in satellite regions, in much the same way that the collapse of the Roman Empire in Europe allowed the rise of the Anglo-Saxon kingdoms in England.

Each of the three states developed its own distinctive culture and art styles. Koguryo grew large and powerful in the 4th and 5th centuries, expanding into Manchuria to the north and beating off massive Chinese invasions under the Sui. Silla in the south developed into a strong kingdom under King Pophung, who instituted a Chinese-style bureaucracy allied to a kinship ranking system known as *kolp'um*, the "hallowed bone" system, where rank was determined by proximity to royal blood. Eventually Silla allied with the new Tang Dynasty in China, and conquered the whole Korean peninsula, establishing the Kingdom of Unified Silla in 668.

▼ This mural from a 4th-century tomb in Koguryo, depicting a lady with her maids, reflects Chinese influence.

4

U.S. presidents assassinated

Four presidents of the United States of America have been assassinated, along with several attempted assassinations on others. The four men to have been shot in office are Abraham Lincoln (d. April 14th, 1865), James Garfield (d. July 2nd, 1881), William McKinley (d. September 6th, 1901), and John F. Kennedy (d. November 22nd, 1963).

A death foretold

The first of these, Abraham Lincoln, was known to be at great risk from potential assassins, and his murder was attended by many ominous portents and missed chances to prevent it. According to a tale told by Lincoln's friend Ward Hill Lamon, just a few days before his death the president dreamed that he stumbled upon a wake in the White House, and when he asked who had died, was told "The president. He was killed by an assassin."

On April 14th Lincoln was in buoyant mood, as the Confederate general Robert E. Lee had recently surrendered and the Civil War was reaching its conclusion. The newspapers reported that the president and his wife would that evening watch a performance of the comedic play *Our American Cousin* at the Ford Theater in Washington, D.C., and despite pleas from his wife and bodyguard not to attend—not least on the grounds that he was a marked man—Lincoln insisted. Arriving after the show had started, Lincoln, his wife, and guests, Major Henry Rathbone and fiancée, took

▲ Abraham Lincoln, captured in 1858 by an early form of photography.

their seats in a box. The policeman who was supposed to guard the door sloped off to a saloon for a drink, and during the third act John Wilkes Booth, a Confederate sympathizer, stepped into the box and leveled his derringer at Lincoln's head.

Rathbone recalled, "I heard the discharge of a pistol behind me, and, looking round, saw through the smoke a man between the door and the President... At the same time I heard the man shout some word, which I thought was 'Freedom!'" Pulling out a knife, Booth slashed at Rathbone, leaped down onto the stage, and escaped through a side door. Rathbone, "then turned to the President; his position was not changed; his head was slightly bent forward and his eyes were closed." Lincoln had been shot through the brain; he did not recover consciousness and died the next day. His wife, Mary Todd, supposedly exclaimed, "His dream was prophetic!"

Death by doctor

President James A. Garfield died as the result of a wound inflicted by an assassin's bullet on July 2nd, 1881, but he did not actually pass away until September 19th, and his death is widely blamed on the ignorance and incompetence of the medical profession. The assassin struck when Garfield was making his way through a train station in Washington, D.C. According to a contemporary account, "While [he was] passing through the ladies' waiting-room two pistol shots were heard in quick succession, one of which took effect in the President's back. He sank to the door, bleeding profusely" and exclaimed "My God, what is this?" The shooter turned out be one Charles J. Guiteau, a disappointed applicant for a government post, of whom Garfield had never even heard.

The gunshot wound was painful but widely believed not to be mortal. But almost immediately doctors set about worsening Garfield's condition. Constant probing of the wound to attempt to locate the bullet led to its becoming much enlarged and infected. By the time of his death a 3-inch (7.5-cm) wound had become a suppurating 20-inch (50-cm) gash. The president wasted from 210 lb (95 kg) to just 130 lb (59 kg). At one point celebrated

▼ The official presidential portrait of James A. Garfield, 20th U.S. president.

inventor Alexander Graham Bell was brought in to use his "induction balance"—a kind of early metal detector—to find the bullet, but without success. Garfield finally died, in great pain, of a heart attack.

"Oh be careful"

William McKinley was shot while visiting the Pan-American Exposition at Buffalo, New York, on September 6th, 1901. He agreed to meet well-wishers and shake hands at the Exposition's Temple of Music, overruling an aide who was concerned at the security risk. "No one would wish to hurt me," demurred McKinley, but he was wrong. Also at the Exposition was anarchist Leon Czolgosz, nursing a grievance over the president's treatment of striking miners back in 1897. Reporter John D. Wells was there: "Suddenly I saw a hand shoved toward the President—two of them in fact—as if the person wished to grasp the president's hand in both his own. In the palm of one hand, the right one, was a handkerchief. Then there were two shots in rapid succession, the interval being so short as to be scarcely measurable."

▲ William McKinley, the 25th president.

The second shot hit McKinley in the stomach and he fell backward as security tackled the gunman. "Be careful how you tell [my wife], oh be careful," he beseeched attendants. Gangrene carried him off eight days later, on September 14th. Czolgosz was executed by electric chair on October 29th.

A drift of blossoms

Perhaps the most infamous presidential assassination is that of John F. Kennedy, on November 22nd, 1963. Three years into his presidency, and approaching reelection, Kennedy was on a politically motivated trip to Dallas. Riding in an open-top car with his wife, Jackie, and the Governor of Texas, John Connally, and his wife Nellie, the president waved to crowds lining the streets. Riding in the car behind were Vice-President Lyndon B. Johnson and his wife Lady Bird, along with Texas Democratic Senator Ralph Yarborough.

At 12:30 the motorcade turned left in front of the Texas School Book Depository building. Lady Bird Johnson recorded her version of events just a few days later, recalling that "Almost at the edge of town... we were rounding a curve, going down a hill, and suddenly there was a sharp, loud report—a shot. It seemed to me to come from the right above my shoulder from a building. Then a moment and then two more shots in rapid succession." Her initial thought was that someone was letting off firecrackers, but the Secret Service threw them to the floor and their car accelerated away. "Only [when we arrived at the hospital] did I believe that this might be what it was. Yarborough kept saying in an excited voice, 'Have they shot the President?' I said something like, 'No, it can't be.'.... I cast one last look over my shoulder and saw, in the President's car, a bundle of pink just like a drift of blossoms, lying on the back seat. I think it was Mrs. Kennedy lying over the President's body."

Kennedy had been shot through the head, while Governor Connally was also wounded. According to the official version, the assassin was a lone gunman named Lee Harvey Oswald, who was apprehended after killing a police officer, and was himself shot dead by Jack Ruby just two days later. But the death of the president gave rise to a vast industry of conspiracy theories, featuring an incredible range of culprits, the more plausible of which include Cuban secret agents sent by Fidel Castro; disaffected anti-Communist Cuban exiles upset by Kennedy's lack of support for the Bay of Pigs invasion fiasco; the Mafia; and Lyndon Johnson himself staging a coup.

▼ John and Jackie Kennedy in the Dallas motorcade, accompanied in the presidential Lincoln Continental by Governor Connally and his wife Nellie.

5

The Five Dynasties and
Ten Kingdoms period
of Chinese history

Just as the collapse of the lengthy Han Dynasty led to a period of instability in which no single state could control all of China, so the breakdown of the Tang Dynasty led to the Five Dynasties and Ten Kingdoms period. Between 907 and the rise of the Song (960), five short-lived dynasties came and went in the north of China, while during roughly the same period the south was split into nine kingdoms, with a tenth small kingdom in the far north.

In 874, after climate change led to a decline in Chinese agricultural production by as much as half, the Huang Chao rebellion sacked the Tang Dynasty's capital cities and fatally weakened the imperial clan. With territory increasingly controlled by local warlords, 907 saw the last Tang emperor deposed by the general Zhu Wen. Zhu founded the Hou ("Later") Liang, which was subsequently overthrown by Zhuangzong, who in 923 founded the Hou Tang. This in turn was overthrown by general Gaozu, in alliance with the semi-nomadic Khitan. In 936 Gaozu founded the Hou Jin Dynasty, but when his son refused to continue paying tribute to the Khitan in 946 they invaded and carried him off. The Hou Jin were followed by the Hou Han and then the Hou Zhou, before finally, in 960, yet another general, Zhao Kuangyin (later known as Taizu), founded the Song Dynasty.

Meanwhile, trade, technology, and culture were flourishing in the nine kingdoms to the south: Wu, Nan Tang, Nan Ping, Chu, Early and Late Shu, Min, Nan Han, and Wu-Yue. The tenth kingdom, in the far north, was the Bei ("Northern") Han.

▲ Tang Dynasty sculpture of a civil servant, in his distinctive hat and robes, holding a tablet bearing an official report. In the 10th century the golden age of Tang China gave way to an era of chaos.

5

Kings killed at the Battle of Brunanburh

"Five kings lay on the field of battle, in bloom of youth, pierced with swords," recorded the Anglo-Saxon Chronicle for the year 937, describing the bloody toll of Brunanburh, arguably the defining battle of English history. Alongside the kings lay seven earls and "unnumber'd crowds" of soldiers, making this one of the bloodiest combats ever to take place on British soil.

The battle was fought between the Anglo-Saxon forces of Athelstan, grandson of Alfred the Great, and an alliance of his Viking and Celtic enemies. Alfred had established his line as the preeminent rulers among the Anglo-Saxons, who controlled most of southern and central England, but the Vikings controlled the northern realms of York and Northumberland and coveted the rest of England, while Celtic kings ruled Welsh and Scottish realms. In 928 Athelstan won a victory over Viking York, and Constantine, the king of Alba (in Scotland), grew wary of his increasing domination of Britain. He put together an alliance with the Celtic kingdom of Strathclyde, and with the Viking earls of Northumberland and the Viking king of Dublin, in Ireland.

In 937 the allies marched into Anglo-Saxon lands, prompting the Anglo-Saxon kingdoms to rally under Athelstan's banner. At Brunanburh the Vikings and Celts were crushed. Athelstan was now firmly established as the king of a united Anglo-Saxon realm, and as overlord of Britain, while the Celts would henceforth be confined within the borders of Wales and Scotland. Brunanburh can thus be said to mark the birth of the English nation.

▲ Late Victorian imagining of Athelstan, first king of all England.

5

South American nations liberated by Simón Bolívar

Simón Bolívar was known as "the Liberator" for his leading part in the independence struggles of many former Spanish colonies in South America, helping to found the republics of Venezuela, Colombia, Ecuador, Peru, and Bolivia during the Wars of Independence (1810–25).

The Napoleonic conquest of Spain saw the installment of Joseph Bonaparte (Napoleon's brother) as King of Spain and sparked revolt in Venezuela, then a Spanish colony. Simón Bolívar was a well-educated young man from a wealthy creole family in Caracas. In 1810 he was sent to London to seek British backing for the independence movement, returning without foreign aid but having recruited expatriate Venezuelan soldier Francisco de Miranda to lead the struggle.

Letter from Jamaica

Bolívar fought under Miranda but the First Republic of Venezuela, declared in 1811, soon fell and Bolívar became the leader of the continuing struggle. The Second Republic, declared in 1813, fell under the onslaught of the *llaneros* (plainsmen)—a potent cavalry force—and after yet another failed revolt Bolívar was forced into exile in Jamaica, where he wrote his seminal *"Carta de Jamaica"* ("Letter from Jamaica"), setting out his vision of a united republican Latin America constituted along British and American lines.

Rebuilding his forces and consolidating patriot factions under his leadership, Bolívar launched a more successful campaign in 1817. By 1819 he was able to declare the Venezuelan Third Republic, and in 1821 he liberated the territory of New Granada at the Battle of Boyacá, followed by a definitive victory over royalist forces in Venezuela at the Battle of Carabobo in 1822. By this time Bolívar had forged the liberated territories of what would later become Ecuador, Colombia, and Venezuela, along with parts of what are now Brazil, Panama, and other countries, into the Republic of Gran Colombia, with himself as its president.

▼ Simón José Antonio de la Santísima Trinidad Bolívar y Palacios, from a posthumous portrait of 1895.

Plowing the sea

Having established Bogotá as the capital of his new state, Bolívar set off to liberate further territories. Between 1822 and 1825 the territories of Quito, Upper Peru (which became Bolivia), and the Viceroyalty of Peru were liberated. The Wars of Independence were now won, but even as he achieved the height of his glory Bolívar was unable to secure the peace. Tensions flared between separatist factions in Caracas and Bogotá, and suspicion grew regarding the extent of Bolívar's pursuit of power.

Bolívar was forced to return to Bogotá to oversee constitutional negotiations between pro- and anti-Bolivarians, and when these broke down in 1828 he assumed dictatorial powers. Within a month, however, he avoided an assassination attempt and was forced into exile. He died in 1830, broken and disillusioned, lamenting that "Those who have served the cause of the revolution have plowed the sea." Gran Colombia quickly broke up into Ecuador, Venezuela, and Colombia. Little over a decade later, however, the rehabilitation of Bolívar's reputation began. Adopted as both nationalist icon and pan-Latin American hero, Bolívar quickly became a near-messianic figure.

5

Archers to each man-at-arms in the English army at Agincourt

The Battle of Agincourt was one of the greatest victories in English military history and was arguably the death knell for a style of combat and the entire socioeconomic system that followed from it. In the fall of 1415 the new king of England, Henry V, invaded France to press his claims to the French throne. His campaign went poorly and his army dwindled, and at Agincourt on October 24th Henry found himself facing a far superior force. The next day battle was joined and Henry's 8,000 men inflicted terrible carnage on the French, killing as many as 10,000 for the loss of around 1,000 of his own men.

The key to the success of Henry's army was its high proportion of archers, who outnumbered the more conventional men-at-arms by five to one. These archers were longbowmen, capable of accurate fire at ranges of up to 200 yards (182 m). Equipped with armor-piercing arrows, and employed with the right tactics on a favorable battlefield, the English longbows were devastating against the heavily armored knights, the combat style characteristic of the feudal nobility. The elite status of the feudal nobles derived from their warrior prowess, which in turn derived from their ability to afford expensive plate armor and horses, which in turn depended on their elite status, so that the feudal aristocracy became a self-sustaining system. The cheaper and therefore more democratic longbow threatened to undermine this system, foreshadowing the dramatic military and socioeconomic consequences of the introduction of gunpowder weapons.

5

Towers of Angkor Wat

Angkor Wat is the greatest and best known of the many temples of Angkor, the capital of the Khmer kingdom in what is now Cambodia. From 889 CE the Khmer kings began to transform Angkor into a earthly representation of Hindu cosmology, and this continued during the reign of Suryavarman II (reigned 1113–1150), who built Angkor Wat, possibly intending it to be his mausoleum. According to an inscription in the temple, Suryavarman II came to power after defeating a rival in single combat, having leaped onto his war elephant.

Angkor Wat was modeled on the topography of the mythical sacred Hindu mountain, Mount Meru, with its five peaks. Accordingly Angkor Wat has five towers, the central one rising to a height of 213 feet (65 m). The temple site itself covers an area of about 500 acres (200 hectares), and is surrounded by a colossal moat, 650 feet (200 m) wide, over 3 miles (5 km) around, and 13 feet (4 m) deep. Digging out the moat meant shifting 53 million cubic feet (1.5 million cubic meters) of sand and silt. The moat stabilizes the temple by regulating the groundwater level.

Hydrological engineering was crucial to the fabric and survival of the great city of Angkor, which may have covered a vast area of up to 400 square miles (1,000 sq km)—possibly even more—making it the largest city in preindustrial history.

▼ One of the five towers of Angkor Wat, representing one of the peaks of the sacred mountain, Meru.

6

Wage that prompted the Tolpuddle Martyrs to organize (shillings)

In 1834 George Loveless, his brother James, James Brine, James Hammet, Thomas Standfield, and his son John, six agricultural laborers from the village of Tolpuddle in Dorset, in southwest England, formed a trade union in a desperate attempt to halt the slide in their wages. A repressive and reactionary state, fearful of labor unrest, convicted them on trumped-up charges and sentenced them to seven years' transportation to Australia: thus was born the legend of the Tolpuddle Martyrs.

Captain Swing revolts

In the early 19th century the agricultural working class suffered from terrible economic hardships. Changes in land rights and increasing mechanization reduced living standards while at the same time driving down wages, and workers had few legitimate means to defend their interests. To sustain even the most meager existence on the breadline a family needed to spend around 14 shillings a week—just over US$1 (about 70p) in today's money. By 1834 the Tolpuddle men had seen their wages cut to starvation levels of just nine shillings a week, and were facing a third cut that would reduce their pay to just six shillings a week: less than 50 cents in modern American currency (~30p in sterling).

A few years earlier a combination of low wages, rising unemployment, severe winters, and poor harvests had resulted in an explosion of civic unrest in the English countryside, known as

▲ Four of the Tolpuddle Martyrs, after an illustration originally in *Cleave's Penny Gazette*.

the Swing Rebellion. In November 1830 desperate workers, angry at the impact of new machines, started smashing threshing machines, burning farm buildings, and assaulting local lawmen. Calling cards were left, attributing the riots to a fictional ringleader, Captain Swing. The authorities responded with an iron fist: 600 Swing rioters were locked up, 500 sentenced to penal transportation, and 19 executed.

Union men

The Tolpuddle men were intent on following a different path to protest, looking to the nascent trade union movement for inspiration. On the advice of the Grand National Consolidated Trades Union they decided to form a union of their own. Meeting under an old sycamore tree or at the house of James Loveless, the six men paid a shilling each and swore before a picture of a skeleton never to divulge the union's secrets.

Local squire and landowner James Frampton, a violent reactionary, despised what he considered to be dangerous revolutionary enthusiasms. He was spying on the Tolpuddle men and connived with local magistrates and the government, fearful of renewed Swing-style unrest, to arrest them on charges of "administering unlawful oaths." Although the statute in question related to naval matters, the trial was hopelessly rigged; the Grand Jury that convicted the men included Frampton and his son and brother, and the brother-in-law of the Home Secretary.

Liberty the watchword

The conclusion of the trial saw the men sentenced to seven years' penal transportation—effectively a one-way ticket given the appalling conditions in the Antipodean penal colonies (see page 120). In response, a massive campaign of protests and agitation across the country transformed the six men into the Tolpuddle Martyrs, and in 1836 the government remitted the sentence. Five of the six men emigrated to Canada; only one returned to live in Tolpuddle.

6

Wives of Henry VIII

Probably the most famous serial husband in history, Henry VIII had six wives between 1509 and his death in 1547, the most of any English king. A combination of lust, superstition, desire to produce a male heir, diplomacy, and obstetric complications lay behind his numerous betrothals and breakups.

Heir loss

In 1509 Henry was married to Katherine of Aragon, a Spanish princess formerly married to Henry's older brother, Arthur, who had died in 1502. Although at first the marriage seemed happy, a series of stillbirths and infant deaths meant that the couple were unable to produce the male heir that Henry craved and needed. By 1526 he had become infatuated with Anne Boleyn, who supposedly refused to sleep with him unless they were married. Henry applied to the Pope for an annulment of his marriage to Katherine on the basis that her previous marriage to his brother invalidated their own betrothal.

Political considerations meant that a papal annulment was not forthcoming, so Henry determined to break with Rome and in 1533 married Anne. In May of that year his new Archbishop of Canterbury, Thomas Cranmer, declared that Henry's marriage to Katherine had been invalid and that his new marriage was valid. Anne was crowned Queen Consort on June 1st, 1533, and in September gave birth to Henry's second daughter, Elizabeth.

▲ Holbein's 1537 portrait of Henry VIII is a political statement in its own right, in which the king is portrayed as physically imposing and richly appareled.

The mare of Flanders

When Anne too proved unable to produce a male heir, Henry
tired of her. Their marriage was annulled and she was convicted
of various crimes, including incest, and beheaded in May 1536.
Just a few weeks later, Henry married Jane Seymour, who had
been one of Anne's ladies-in-waiting, but she died a few days after
giving birth to a son, who would later become Edward VI. Henry's
next wife, chosen for political reasons, was Anne of Cleves, a
German princess, but according to popular legend Henry was
so dismayed by her appearance that he called her "a Flanders'
mare." Their marriage was annulled in July 1540 after just six
months, but since she did not oppose the dissolution she was
given a generous settlement and remained on friendly terms
with Henry (becoming known as "the King's Sister").

In July 1540 Henry married Catherine Howard, but in
November of the following year she was found guilty of adultery
with Thomas Culpeper and beheaded in February 1542. Henry's
last wife was Catherine Parr, a twice-widowed noblewoman
credited with restoring stability to his court and family. Parr
outlived Henry, who died in 1547, but after remarrying she died,
probably from complications in childbirth, in September 1548.

Aides mémoire

A common mnemonic device for the fates of Henry's six wives is the short rhyme "divorced,
beheaded, died; divorced, beheaded, survived." In fact divorce was not available at the time,
and four of Henry's marriages were annulled. Remembering the names of the six wives has
challenged schoolchildren for generations, particularly given the preponderance of K/
Catherines. One helpful mnemonic is:

Arrogant	Anne	Seemed More	Clever	At How to	Catch The Ring
Katherine of Aragon	Anne Boleyn	Jane Seymour	Anne of Cleves	Catherine Howard	Catherine Parr

6

The Six-Day War

The Six-Day War of 1967 was a conflict between Israel and its Arab neighbors, Egypt, Jordan, Syria, and the Palestinians. The roots of the conflict lay in a complex brew of tensions between Israel and its neighbors, between the neighbors themselves, and between the rival superpowers, the USSR and the USA.

In the Suez Crisis of 1956, Israel, with Anglo-French support, had conquered Egypt's Sinai peninsula, only to be forced to back down by international pressure. The following year Israel withdrew from Sinai, on the basis that UN peacekeeping forces would safeguard Israeli maritime access through the Straits of Tiran. After an initial surge in popularity, Egyptian president Gamal Abdel Nasser's prestige declined and a short-lived union with Syria fell apart, and he lost face in the Arab world for perceived weakness in dealings with Israel. He had lost American support and in its place Egypt had become a client state of the Soviets. Meanwhile increasingly militant agitation by Palestinians in Jordan had destabilized the country and made it a target for Israeli reprisals.

In 1966 Palestinians in Jordan launched attacks across the frontier, and by 1967 tension in the region was very high, with spurious reports of Syrian mobilization on the Israeli border. The tipping point came in May, when Nasser ordered UN forces to leave the Sinai and declared that Israeli vessels could no longer pass the Straits of Tiran. Convinced that war was now inevitable, Israel launched a preemptive strike.

On June 5th one of the most devastating
and successful military campaigns of the
modern era began, and within three hours the
war's outcome was decided. Israeli warplanes,
armed with excellent intelligence and the
crucial knowledge that Egyptian planes
returned to base every morning at 7 am for
breakfast, destroyed the air forces of Egypt,
Jordan, and Syria. In just a few hours all 17
Egyptian air bases were attacked and 300
combat aircraft were destroyed on the
ground. The Jordanian air force was
completely wiped out and the Syrian air
force crippled.

With no air cover, Arab armor was
defenseless. First the Israelis dealt with the
Egyptians. They captured the Gaza Strip on
June 6th and marched into Sinai, routing
seven Egyptian divisions and killing 15,000
men, reaching the Suez Canal by June 9th.
Jordanian forces were defeated even more
quickly, and by June 7th Jordan had lost the
old city of Jerusalem and the West Bank.
Egypt and Jordan quickly accepted UN
demands for a ceasefire, and Israel was able
to concentrate its forces on Syria, taking the
Golan Heights on the border and advancing to within range of
Damascus. Syria accepted a ceasefire on June 10th.

This lightning victory left Israel with several occupied territories,
and their hundreds of thousands of restive inhabitants, while the
Palestinian refugee crisis in neighboring states intensified. Egypt's
economy was left in tatters and Nasser resigned. The Soviets
intensified their support for Egypt, but perhaps most significantly
the Six-Day War convinced the Americans that Israel could be a
powerful bulwark against Soviet influence in the region, and they
began to pour money and arms into the country, cementing the
now entrenched special relationship between America and Israel.

▲ On land and at sea, Israeli
forces battled on several
fronts, but the crucial success
came in the brief air war.

7

Voyages of Zheng He

During China's Ming Dynasty, Zheng He was a Chinese Muslim eunuch who became a powerful courtier and was put in charge of a series of enormous and powerful fleets that undertook voyages of exploration, trade, and power projection around the Indian Ocean. He made seven voyages, starting in 1405 and ending in 1433, when he died on his way back to China.

Zheng He (born as Ma He) was captured in Yunnan and taken into service at the imperial court as a eunuch, distinguishing himself in the military service of Prince Zhu Di, who in 1402 would become the Yongle Emperor. Ma received the honorific "Zheng," possibly as the result of exploits at the Battle of Zhenglunba. The Yongle emperor had expansionist and internationalist ambitions, and put Zheng He in charge of preparing and overseeing a huge fleet of 300 ships and 25,000 men.

The first voyage (1405-07) visited Java, Sumatra, and Sri Lanka, reaching as far as the Malabar coast of India, and battled pirates in the Strait of Malacca. The second voyage (1407-09) visited Thailand and India. The third (1409-11) toured Southeast Asia and southwest India and Sri Lanka. The fourth and greatest expedition (1413-15) visited Calicut in India and reached Hormuz on the Persian Gulf, sending ships to explore the East African coast as far as Mogadishu in Somalia and Malindi in Kenya.

So many envoys returned to China with Zheng He that a fifth expedition (1417-19) was dispatched to take them home; this again ventured as far as East Africa. The sixth voyage (1421-22) again

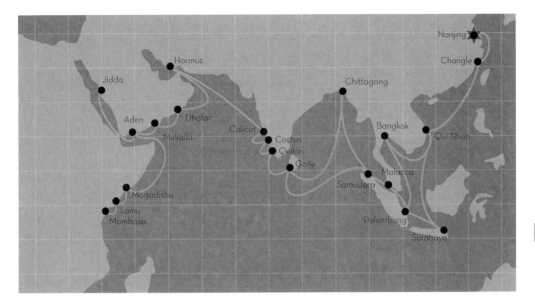

reached the Somali coast, but back in China the Yongle emperor was mired in grand projects and economic and military complications, and it was not until the accession of a later ruler, the Xuande Emperor, that Zheng He was sent on his seventh and last voyage (1431–33), in the course of which he died.

▲ Ships under Zheng He's command visited almost every corner of the Indian Ocean, from southern Indonesia to the Red Sea to the East African coast, although the exact routes followed by the different parts of his fleets are not known.

Sails like clouds

The achievements of Zheng He's fleets and his voyages are remarkable. His fourth fleet, for instance, included 63 great ships of up to 260 ft (80 m) in length—possibly longer. "Our sails, loftily unfurled like clouds," boasted a contemporary account of Zheng He's voyages, "day and night continued their course as rapidly as a star, traversing the savage waves as if we were treading a public thoroughfare… We have beheld in the ocean huge waves like mountains rising sky high, and we have set eyes on barbarian regions far away…" After Zheng He's death the Ming Dynasty retreated into an isolationist policy; his logbooks were burned and maritime trade was eventually outlawed. China's absence from the high seas left a vacuum soon filled by the Europeans.

7

Cities of Cíbola

The Seven Cities of Cíbola were legendary Christian kingdoms of fabulous wealth believed by Spanish explorers of the 16th century to be hidden deep in the North American interior; northern analogs of South America's El Dorado. The evolution of their legend traces the retreating frontiers of European exploration of the Atlantic and the New World, inspiring extraordinary feats of discovery and cruelty.

The Blessed Isles

Since Greek and Roman times the Atlantic was believed to harbor magical lands and islands, variously known as the Blessed Isles, Hy-Brasil, and Antillia. These legends became conflated with an Iberian folk tradition that, following the Moorish conquest of Iberia, seven bishops and their flocks had sailed westward across the ocean to settle new lands and establish a flourishing commonwealth of seven city-states, depicted as a Christian utopia of wealth and magnificence. These Seven Cities of Gold were assumed to lie on the island of Antillia, a landmass routinely depicted on maps of the Atlantic. Sailors' tales told of sighting the island and one legend spoke of a captain who landed and found the sand of its beaches was two-thirds gold dust. Columbus expected to stop at Antillia en route to the Indies.

Black Stephen

Exploration of the Atlantic revealed no trace of the Seven Cities of Gold, although islands in the West Indies were named the Antilles. Instead, the location of these legendary honeypots shifted west, especially when survivors of a disastrous 1528 expedition into the North American interior brought back tales of fabulous Indian cities. One of these survivors, a Moorish slave called Estebanico (a Spanish variant of the English name Stephen, so that he is also known as Black Stephen), became the first named black African to play a part in North American history. Estebanico had gifts for language and medicine, and became known among the Native American tribes as a healer. He served as a trailblazer for an *entrada*—a Spanish expedition of discovery conquest, and looting—leaving a trail of crosses for the *entrada* to follow, and a message that spoke of seven great cities of the Indians, the greatest of which was the fabulously wealthy Cíbola.

Dreams of gold

Another, even greater *entrada* was launched to investigate—and plunder—what the Spanish assumed to be the *Sete Cidades* of legend. Led by Don Francisco Vásquez de Coronado, this famous expedition sighted the Grand Canyon and reached as far as Kansas, but Coronado's dreams of gold were dashed. The "fabulous cities" of the Indians turned out to be the Pueblos of the Zuni Indians and other "Pueblo Peoples," building complexes constructed from adobe. Supposedly the golden glitter of the earlier sightings could be explained by the sun glinting off the straw in the adobe. Contact with the Spanish ultimately proved disastrous for the Pueblo Peoples, and they were cruelly treated and largely wiped out in later years.

▼ Coronado exploring the American Midwest, accompanied by native guides and would-be conquistadors.

7

Chicago peace protestors arrested in wake of Democratic Convention riots

The Chicago Seven, originally the Chicago Eight, were a group of peace protestors and countercultural figures charged with conspiracy to commit a riot in the aftermath of the violence surrounding the 1968 Democratic National Convention (DNC) in Chicago. The original eight men were Rennie Davis, David Dellinger, John Froines, Tom Hayden, Abbie Hoffman, Jerry Rubin, Bobby Seale, and Lee Weiner. Bobby Seale was cofounder of the Black Panthers, an organization that had been only peripherally involved in the DNC protests, and after a dramatic incident in which the judge ordered him to be bound and gagged in court, he was sentenced to four years in prison for contempt of court and the trial of the other seven defendants went on without him.

The case appeared to be an establishment attempt to put the Sixties counterculture itself on trial (particularly given that the DNC violence was largely down to what a federal commission later called "a police riot"). Defendants such as Abbie Hoffman used the trial as a stage for provocative performance art/ ideological grandstanding. The defense called as witnesses a colorful cast of counter-culture characters, including poet Allen Ginsberg, folk singer Pete Seeger, and novelist Norman Mailer.

The judge refused to allow the defense to select the jury fairly, and five of the seven were found guilty, while all of them and their lawyers were pronounced guilty of 175 counts of contempt of court and given harsh sentences. The verdicts and most of the contempt charges were overturned on appeal.

7

Length of the first
global war (years)

The Seven Years' War, the North American theater of which is known as the French and Indian War, was the first world war, drawing in most of the great powers of Europe and raging across the globe from Quebec to India. It proved pivotal for the next century and a half of history, confirming Prussia as a major force in Europe and the leading power in Germany, and Britain as a world empire destined to become a global superpower.

Diplomatic revolution

The roots of the war lay in ongoing tension between Britain and Bourbon France. France was the most powerful country in Europe, and Britain was increasingly concerned to limit its growing colonial ambitions, while furthering its own. Forces of the two countries clashed in North America in 1755, and war between them loomed. Worried about the vulnerability to French attacks of his Hanoverian possessions in Germany, in 1756 the British king George II concluded a treaty with Frederick II of Prussia. This in turn helped to hasten the conclusion of ongoing talks between Austria and France, and in 1756 they formed an alliance in what was known as "the diplomatic revolution." They were soon joined by Russia, Sweden, and other nations.

Aware that his enemies' alliance encircled his precariously placed state, and believing strongly in aggression and initiative in military strategy, Frederick struck first, invading Saxony in 1756 to remove it from play. The following year Prussia invaded Bohemia but was checked and thrown back by Austrian forces. Using his interior lines to good effect, Frederick concentrated his forces on first one enemy and then another, winning great victories against the French at Rossbach in November 1757, and against the Austrians at Leuthen in December. Bloody battles in 1758 checked a Russian invasion of Prussia.

In Britain, William Pitt the Elder had become Prime Minister, adopting a policy of funding mercenary armies against France on the Continent while pursuing the war overseas through the Navy, expeditionary forces and local militia. British-funded armies won victories in Europe in 1758 and 1759, but Frederick was suffering terrible casualties in battles against the Austrians and Russians. Although he chased a Russian army out of Berlin in October 1760 and gained a costly victory over the Austrians at Torgau in November, Frederick's position worsened, especially when Pitt lost power in 1761 and his subsidies dried up.

▲ Pitt the Elder, whose hawkish policy saw Britain taking on France at sea and on land, albeit through proxies such as Prussia.

All around the world

Meanwhile the British Navy had foiled French invasion plans by pounding their fleet off Lagos in Portugal in August 1759 and in Quiberon Bay off Brittany in November. British naval forces also captured a string of colonial outposts around the world, including significant victories over the French in Quebec (1759) and Montreal (1760)—which brought Canada into British hands and made the French presence in North America ultimately untenable—and over the French at Pondicherry in India in 1761, opening the way for the East India Company to begin extending its power across the entire subcontinent. When Spain, under its Bourbon rulers, entered the war on the side of France in 1761, the British took Gibraltar, Manila, and Cuba, which they later traded for Florida. The British also conquered Grenada, Martinique, and Guadeloupe, and took French bases in West Africa.

In Europe things looked grim for Frederick, but in 1762 he was saved by the death of one of his most implacable foes, Tsarina Elizabeth of Russia. Her successor, Peter III, was an ardent admirer of Frederick and Prussia, and promptly agreed a peace treaty relinquishing all Russian conquests. Peter was soon assassinated, but by then the threat to Prussia had passed. Vast stores of blood and treasure had been expended—Prussia had lost around 500,000 men, while Austria, Russia, and France had each lost around 300,000—and in 1763 the war-weary powers agreed peace treaties at Hubertusburg and Paris. The result of these was mostly a return to the prewar status quo, except that Prussia gained Silesia, a rich territory that would later be key to its economic strength, and Britain gained a string of territories and important bases across the world. British naval supremacy was confirmed and its empire was now set to expand dramatically. With the French threat to the American colonies now extinguished, however, the common enemy that had bound British and colonial interests was gone. Thus were set in motion events leading to the Revolution and American independence.

▼ Benjamin West's *Death of General Wolfe* shows the last moments of Britain's greatest military hero of the 18th century, at the Battle of Quebec in September 1759.

9

Crusades

In 1056 the Great Schism had divided the Eastern and Western Churches, while in 1071 Jerusalem had been taken by the Seljuk Turks, who also made inroads into the shrinking Byzantine Empire. Europe was experiencing population growth and increasing prosperity, while its warrior nobility class engaged in constant internecine warfare. Pope Urban II saw a chance to channel the energy of European feudalism into an expedition that might bring the East once more under the aegis of Rome, and at the Council of Clermont in 1095, he preached a new holy war, or crusade, to a largely Frankish audience.

The First Crusade

There was great enthusiasm for this new venture, partly out of religious zeal, but also for economic and political reasons. There were new lands and treasures to be won, trade routes to control, and indulgences on offer. First to answer the call was a motley collection of peasants, whose Paupers' Crusade quickly ended in tragedy, death, and enslavement. Knights of France and Lorraine were much better organized—other nations were hostile,

▼ Timeline showing the Crusades. Their numbering can vary depending on how some of the minor military ventures are rated.

1090   1100   1110   1120   1130   1140   1150   1160   1170   118

indifferent, or otherwise occupied—and three groups of Crusaders under Godfrey and Baldwin of Bouillon, Count Raymond of Toulouse, and the Norman Bohemund of Otranto, launched the First Crusade.

Muslim forces in the Near East were in disarray and struggled to cope with the unfamiliar challenge of battling heavily armored knights, and the Crusaders scored a string of successes. In 1097 they captured the Seljuk Rum capital of Nicaea and conquered Edessa; in 1098 they took Antioch after a long siege; and in 1099 they captured Jerusalem. Four Crusader kingdoms were established: the kingdom of Jerusalem; the county of Tripoli; the county of Edessa, established by Baldwin; and the principality of Antioch. New orders of knights, the Hospitallers and the Templars, helped maintain the military might of the Crusaders.

▲ Detail from a 14th-century manuscript miniature, showing Philip II of France disembarking in the Holy Land during the Third Crusade.

Rise of the Zengids

Further campaigns in the early 12th century helped enlarge and consolidate these kingdoms, but in 1144 a new dynasty, the Zengids, rose out of Mosul and conquered Edessa. This prompted the Second Crusade, launched in 1147 under Conrad III of Germany and Louis VII of France, but it went badly awry. Both kings lost most of their forces en route to the Holy Land, and instead of attacking the Zengids they instead attacked the Burids in Damascus—the only Islamic state friendly to the Crusaders. Their siege failed and the Second Crusade broke up having achieved nothing. The rise of the Zengids continued and the Crusader kingdoms inexorably declined.

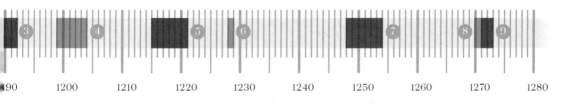

3		4		5	6			7		8	9	
90	1200	1210	1220	1230	1240	1250	1260	1270	1280

In the 1180s the Zengid leader Saladin began to unite the disparate Muslim states under his banner, but maintained an uneasy truce with the leper king of Jerusalem, Baldwin IV. When Baldwin died, however, conflict flared up and at the Horns of Hattin, in 1187, the Crusaders suffered a crushing and bloody defeat. The way was clear for Saladin to take Acre and Jerusalem in short order, leaving only a few city-states as all that remained of Outremer (the kingdom "beyond the sea").

The Latin Empire

The fall of Jerusalem precipitated the Third Crusade, under Richard the Lionheart of England and Philip II Augustus of France, in 1190; the German emperor Frederick Barbarossa drowned while traveling through Turkey. Although Richard never lost a battle in the Holy Land, he was unable to retake Jerusalem. He did help reconquer Acre (after which the Crusaders massacred most of the population), and take Cyprus from the Byzantines, selling it to the Templars, who used it as one of the main supports for the ongoing Christian presence in Outremer, now restricted to a long, thin strip of coastline from Tyre to Jaffa, along with Antioch and Tripoli (in what is now Lebanon). The failure of the Third Crusade led Pope Innocent III to proclaim a Fourth Crusade in 1199, with disastrous consequences, for the Crusaders got no further than Constantinople. In 1204 they sacked the city and established a short-lived Latin Empire there, fatally weakening the Byzantine Empire.

The Holy Land was not the only target of the Crusader movement. In 1208 Pope Innocent III proclaimed a crusade against heretics in the south of France—mainly the Albigenses, known as Cathars. The Albigensian Crusade eventually wiped out the Cathars and helped the French kings extend their power across southern France, with Toulouse finally ceded in 1229.

Epic failures

In 1212 the tragic Children's Crusade ended in death and slavery for most of its participants. It was followed in 1215 by the Fifth Crusade, which targeted Egypt but left empty-handed in 1221 after foolishly refusing a treaty that would have given them Jerusalem. Emperor Frederick II made no such mistake in 1229, when he concluded the Sixth Crusade without a single battle, having agreed with the Egyptian sultan a treaty restoring Jerusalem to the Christians, though it was lost for a final time in 1244. In 1248 Louis IX of France took the cross and set out on the Seventh Crusade (or the Eighth, if an earlier effort by Theobald of Navarre is counted). He captured Damietta but in 1250 his army was crushed and he was taken captive and then ransomed.

By 1260 the Mamluks of Egypt had become the preeminent power in the Near East, and set their sights on driving out the Crusaders from their last remaining strongholds. Louis IX's Eighth Crusade ended even more disastrously than the previous one, when he died in Tunis in 1270 without ever having reached the Levant. In the Ninth and final crusade, Edward Plantagenet of England successfully defended Acre from the Mamluks in 1271, but returned home the following year to be crowned king. The treaty he had negotiated expired and in 1291 Acre fell, followed by Beirut, the last remaining Crusader toehold in the Holy Land.

The Mamluks devastated the region to forestall further Crusades, and Europe lost its appetite for Levantine adventures. Energies would instead be focused against the Ottoman Turks as they took the Balkans and advanced on Constantinople.

Nevertheless, despite their ultimate failure, the Crusades stimulated European development through increasing contact with other cultures, with many technological and cultural influences flowing East to West.

▼ In Karl Friedrich Lessing's 1835 painting, *The Last Crusader*, an elderly Templar knight wends his weary way home from the Holy Land.

9

Knights who founded the Templar order

The Templar order was founded in 1118 by French knight Hugues de Payens and eight companions, to help protect pilgrims traveling from Jaffa on the Mediterranean coast to Jerusalem. The order modeled itself on the Cistercians, with vows of poverty, chastity, and obedience, and was assigned quarters in the Temple Mount compound, hence their name. Although poor to begin with, the Templars quickly gained favor and fortune. A special dispensation from the Pope exempted them from taxation, while donations of money and land meant they had holdings across Europe, and developed a banking and shipping service to manage the flow of money and people to and from the Holy Land. Their ranks swelled, with almost 1,000 brother knights by 1170, and up to 10,000 of lower rank. The Templars became one of the primary military forces in Outremer and gained power elsewhere.

The reverses inflicted on the Crusader kingdoms undermined the resources and authority of the Templars, making them vulnerable to the machinations of their enemy Philip IV the Fair, king of France. Compelling papal assent, Philip struck against the order on Friday, October 13th, 1307, arresting every Templar in France. They were accused of various crimes, including heresy, sexual and occult crimes, and devil worship, and over 60 Templars were executed. In 1312 Pope Clement V dissolved the order. Templar imagery and labels were later adopted by Freemasonry and the Templars have since become a mainstay of conspiracy theories and alternative history.

9

Sacks filled to the brim with ears

At the Battle of Liegnitz (modern-day Legnica) in Poland in 1241, a Mongol army destroyed the army of Duke Henry II of Silesia. The Mongol force was part of a larger army sent by Batu, grandson of Genghis Khan and leader of the Golden Horde (the Kipchak Khanate), to devastate and conquer swathes of Europe. While the main Mongol force destroyed the Hungarians at the Battle of Mohi, a smaller force of 20,000 horsemen was sent north, under the leadership of generals Baidar and Kaidu, to cut off reinforcements coming from Poland.

From early March, 1241, the Mongols left a trail of destruction across Poland, defeating armies at Kraków and Chmielnik. Acting on excellent intelligence, they intercepted the most powerful prince in Poland, Henry II, before he could link up with a large army from Bohemia. At Liegnitz, Henry had gathered a 30,000-strong force, which he led out to meet the Mongols (known to the Europeans as "Tatars"). The Mongol light cavalry knew they could not match the heavily armored knights in straight combat; instead they used the false rout, pretending to retreat and luring the knights away from their infantry support before peppering them with arrows from a distance. They also used devices such as smoke screens.

Henry duly led his men into the trap, whereupon they were routed. A contemporary chronicler recorded that "the Tatars, wishing to know the exact number of the dead, cut one ear off each corpse, filling nine huge sacks to the brim."

9/11

Terrorist attacks on the USA

The terrorist attacks of September 11th, 2001, involved hijackers flying commercial jet airplanes full of passengers into the towers of the World Trade Center (WTC) in New York and the Pentagon in Washington, D.C., while a fourth plane crashed into a field in Shanksville, Pennsylvania, probably after the passengers tried to seize control of the plane from the hijackers. The attacks have been compared in impact and consequences to the Pearl Harbor attack of 1941. With around 3,000 fatalities, more lives were lost in 9/11 than at Pearl Harbor; in both cases there is evidence that the government should have done more to heed possible intelligence; and in both cases America's response was to launch a devastating war on multiple fronts.

The attacks were masterminded by the terrorist organization Al Qaeda, under its leader Osama bin Laden, a Saudi national. Bin Laden believed that the lesson of previous terrorist attacks on American interests—in Lebanon, Somalia, and Yemen—was that the Americans would withdraw or retaliate at worst with ineffective cruise missile attacks. Having found a safe haven in Afghanistan, with its sympathetic Taliban regime, Bin Laden adopted a plot formulated by the Kuwaiti Khalid Sheikh Mohammed, using hijackers to take over airliners and fly them into buildings. Al Qaeda provided funding, training, and coordination, recruiting militants such as Mohamed Atta, who would become the operational leader of the plot. Atta and some of the other key terrorists had been educated in the West, becoming radicalized but also more adept at fitting in and moving across borders. Having met in Hamburg, Atta and his group went to Afghanistan in 1999 looking for jihadi training and were promptly recruited by Al Qaeda. Over the next two years they moved to the United States and some received pilot training.

Attack on America

On the morning of September 11th, 19 hijackers in four groups boarded planes at Boston, Washington, D.C., and Newark, targeting large liners loaded with fuel for flights to the West Coast. Using boxcutters, they overpowered and disabled crew members and hijacked the planes. At 8:45 am American Airlines flight 11 from Boston smashed into the north tower of the WTC, and 17 minutes later United Airlines flight 175 from Boston hit the south tower. The explosions and full loads of jet fuel started raging fires. At 9:37 am, American Airlines flight 77 from Dulles Airport plowed into the Pentagon on the outskirts of Washington, D.C., where the impact and subsequent fire killed 184 people, and at 10:03 am, passengers on United Airlines flight 93 from Newark, alerted via cell phone to the likely fate of their aircraft, tried to storm the cockpit, whereupon the hijacker pilot crashed the plane into a field in Pennsylvania, killing all 40 passengers.

By this time the nation's airspace had been closed and all civil aviation was grounded, while President George W. Bush was rushed onto Air Force One to be flown from one site to another. At 9:59 am the south tower of the WTC collapsed, followed by the north tower at 10:28 AM. Around 2,750 people perished at the WTC, including around 400 police and firefighters.

In response the U.S. government introduced new powers for surveillance at home, and started a massive global effort to eliminate Al Qaeda. American forces and their allies toppled the Taliban regime in Afghanistan that had harbored Al Qaeda, and President Bush declared a new doctrine of preemptive attacks against possible enemies of America, which led to the 2003 invasion of Iraq. In 2011 Bin Laden himself was tracked down to a compound in Abbottabad, Pakistan, and killed by special forces.

▲ (Top) The second plane strikes the South Tower. (Middle) Just after the collapse of the second tower. (Bottom) Shattered remnants of the foot of one of the towers.

10

Days that shook the world

Ten Days That Shook the World is the title of a 1919 book by American journalist John Reed, recounting the pivotal days of the November Revolution of 1917 (which Russians, who at that time still used the Old Julian calendar, called the October Revolution). There were three distinct Russian Revolutions in the early 20th century: the Revolution of 1905, the February Revolution of 1917, and the October one. It is this last one that people usually mean when they refer to the Russian Revolution.

The 1905 Revolution, precipitated by the disastrous conduct of the 1904–05 war against Japan, reflected growing discontent at the repressive, corrupt, and incompetent rule of the tsars and the grinding poverty of much of the population. Its primary legacy was the institution of the Duma, the Russian parliament, but most of the population's discontents remained and the even more disastrous conduct of the World War I meant that by 1917 Russia was in turmoil. There were widespread food riots and mutinies among the military, leading to the February Revolution, during which Tsar Nicholas II was forced to abdicate and a Provisional Government was set up by the Duma in Petrograd (formerly St. Petersburg). At the same time workers and soldiers in Petrograd had set up a worker's council or *soviet*, and it was this which controlled transport, troops, and communications. For eight months the Provisional Government and the soviet governed in uneasy alliance, as the latter bided its time before taking full power, while within the soviet the Bolshevik faction strengthened.

▲ Lenin, who wrote the foreword to the second edition of John Reed's seminal book *Ten Days That Shook the World*.

"All Power to the Soviets!"

In April 1917 the Germans allowed Vladimir Lenin to travel to Russia, correctly surmising that he would undermine their enemy's war effort. Lenin galvanized the Bolsheviks and gained the support of the masses through slogans that echoed their primary demands: "Peace, Land, and Bread!" "End the War!" and "All Power to the Soviets!"

After a false start in July, the Bolsheviks, aided by the Red Guard workers' militia and sailors from Kronstadt, executed a coup on the night of October 24th (November 6th), storming the Winter Palace in Petrograd, headquarters of the Provisional Government. The Bolsheviks had extended their control to soviets across European Russia, and these now helped secure strategic posts around the country, seizing telegraph stations and government buildings. On October 25th an All Russian Congress of Soviets was held, from which Trotsky expelled rival factions to the Bolsheviks; the Congress then approved the formation of a new government of Bolshevik commissars, with Lenin at its head.

In the months that followed, Lenin agreed to a humiliating peace deal with Germany, which gave away many non-Russian territories that had already seceded, and Russia was plunged into civil war. John Reed, a socialist American journalist who had followed events closely at first hand, returned to America in April 1918, and after a long battle with suspicious authorities to recover his notes and papers, plunged into the writing of his famous book, now regarded as a masterpiece of engaged long-form journalism. In 1919 Lenin wrote a foreword for the second edition—"unreservedly do I recommend it to the workers of the world"—but under Stalin the book was banned since it made virtually no mention of him, depicting Trotsky as central to the Revolution.

▼ Scene from the Revolution; gunfire scatters civilians in front of the Winter Palace in Petrograd.

12

Number of the Hidden Imam, al-Mahdi

Islam has two primary traditions: Sunni and Shi'ite. The schism between the two dates back to the death of Mohammed, founder of Islam, and the dispute over the succession. Shi'ite Islam arose from those who supported a line of succession descending from the Prophet's cousin and son-in-law Ali Ibn Abi Talib, each of whom were Imams—leaders endowed with divine qualities.

The majority of Shi'ites believe that the eleventh Imam (which is to say, the eleventh in direct descent from the Prophet), Hassan al-Askari, and his family were kept under house arrest by the dominant Sunni faction during the late 9th century. When al-Askari died in 873, his infant son, Mohammed, the Twelfth Imam, was smuggled to freedom and kept hidden. Over the next 70 years the Twelfth Imam became associated among mainstream Shi'ites with the Mahdi, an Islamic messiah figure. In 941 it was said that the Twelfth Imam had disappeared from the earthly realm. The majority of Shi'ite Muslims now believe that the Twelfth, Hidden Imam will reappear as the Mahdi and bring truth and justice to the world.

Belief in the Hidden Imam, the Mahdi, has had major historical ramifications. A number of individuals have been identified with the Mahdi, notably Shah Ismail, leader of the Safavids who conquered Persia in the 16th century, and Muhammad Ahmad (1884–85) who led a "Mahdist" uprising in Anglo-Egyptian Sudan. In Iran, the ruling clerics derive much of their authority from being considered as representatives of the Hidden Imam.

▲ Portrait of Muhammad Ahmad, leader of the Mahdist Revolt against British-backed Egyptian rule of the Sudan in the 1880s.

18

Ife bronze heads

The bronze heads of the Ife are among the most celebrated cultural achievements of West African history. These beautiful sculptures, of which 18 are known today, were probably cast around the 14th century, but they represent a cultural tradition dating back to the 11th century. They are evidence of the prosperity brought to parts of sub-Saharan West Africa during the medieval period, when much of the gold in European and Islamic coinage came from West Africa. Several empires and kingdoms blossomed during this period, including the Yoruba.

Yoruba was the name given by outsiders to a group of city-states in what is now Nigeria, which shared a common language and culture. The cultural and spiritual heartland of the Yoruba region was Ife, a city-state where a sophisticated urban culture emerged by the middle of the 11th century, declining ca. 1500.

The forest kingdom of Ife was connected by trade routes to the dry grassland city-states of Gao and Timbuktu in the north, and the Hausa kingdoms like Kano and the Kanem-Bornu empire in the east. Trade routes also connected West Africa to the Islamic kingdoms of North Africa and the wider world, bringing luxury goods, ideas, and religion. Evidently by around 1400 some group or person in Ife was wealthy and powerful enough to possess valuable bronze and beads and fund a craft tradition capable of making them. Similarities in style suggest that all 18 Ife metal heads may have been made in the same workshop, perhaps by the same person—a Yoruba Ghiberti or Michelangelo?

▼ Although traditionally described as bronze, this Ife head is actually made of a copper alloy more similar to brass.

22

Average age of U.S. combat soldiers in Vietnam

According to a well-known electronic dance song of 1985, "the average age of the combat soldier in Vietnam was 19," in contrast to the average for an American combat soldier in World War II: 26. In fact the claim made in the sample used in the song is probably incorrect.

Although there are no definitive figures, and it depends on what is understood by "combat soldier," the best source is the Combat Area Casualty File (CACF), which was used as the basis for the Vietnam Veterans Memorial in Washington, D.C. According to the CACF, the average age for an American infantryman killed in action was 22 years; assuming that those killed in action represent the demographics of all the combat infantrymen, the 1985 song should be called "22."

For all 58,148 Americans killed in Vietnam for whom there are birth and death dates recorded, the average age was 23.11 years. This is indeed around three years younger than the figure for American combat soldiers in World War II. In addition, over 11,000 American soldiers killed in action were under 20 years of age. Over 2 million Americans served in Vietnam between 1964 and 1973 , with a peak American troop strength in the country of over 500,000 in 1968. The Vietnam War itself is said to have run from 1954 to 1975: from the end of the Indochinese War, in which the Vietnamese drove out the French and the country was divided into North and South, to the eventual fall of Saigon. American involvement had more or less ended, however, in 1973.

▲ Da Nang, Vietnam. A young Marine private waits on the beach during the amphibious landing of August 3rd, 1965.

24

Life expectancy of a Soviet private at Stalingrad (hours)

The Battle of Stalingrad, which raged for 199 days from June 1942 to January 1943, was arguably the worst battle of World War II and possibly the most terrible of all time. The eventual death toll, including combatants and civilians, was around 2 million.

In attacking Stalingrad, Hitler intended to take a strategic city on the Volga, cutting off Soviet supply lines between the north and the breadbasket of the Ukraine and the oilfields of the Caucasus, while simultaneously delivering a major propaganda coup, given that the city was named for Hitler's nemesis. For much the same reasons, Stalin was grimly determined to hold the city.

The initial German advance on Stalingrad was swift, forcing the Russians to scramble a defense amid the ruins of the city center. Stalin ordered that the civilian population must not leave, and poured all available manpower into the city. The Germans had set up artillery positions commanding the river, and they had total air superiority. Soviet reinforcements had to enter the city center by boat, running a gauntlet of shells and bombs.

By July the life expectancy of a newly arrived Soviet infantryman was less than 24 hours: officers could expect to survive for three days. But the terrible sacrifices succeeded in halting the Germans, buying time for the Soviets to organize their counter-offensive, and in November Operation Uranus succeeded in encircling the German 6th Army.

▼ Soldiers in winter camouflage taking up position in the city of Stalingrad, scene of perhaps the worst battle in history.

24

Ships that set out to colonize Greenland

In 986, 24 shiploads of Norse colonists set out from Iceland for Greenland, an island that, despite its name, is almost entirely covered by a vast ice sheet. In one of the most famous instances of canny marketing, it was named by an adventurer, explorer, and sometime outlaw called Eric Thorvaldson, aka Eric the Red.

Eric had been born in Norway around 950, moved to Iceland, and in 982 was exiled from there for three years. He and his followers spent the time exploring the land known to exist to the west of Iceland. In some accounts Eric named the new country Greenland because he genuinely believed it was better suited to farming livestock than Iceland; he evidently considered it a good place to settle, for on returning to Iceland he recruited men and women to return with him and found a new colony.

Of the 24 ships that set out, only 14 arrived, but they succeeded in founding what became a thriving community spread across two settlement areas. Eventually there were around 400 farms, with a peak population of about 5,000, able to build and support a cathedral larger than any in Iceland. Although essentials like timber and iron were in short supply, the Greenlanders carried out a lively trade via visiting Norwegian ships, offering valuables such as walrus ivory, polar bear skins, and narwhal tusks.

Eric died around 1005, not long after his son Leif discovered Newfoundland (which he called Vinland ["Vineland"], having picked up a trick from his father). The Greenland settlement lasted until the late 15th century.

▲ Rather anachronistic 17th-century depiction of Eric the Red. Metal was in short supply in Greenland; such armor would have been much appreciated.

24

Wild rabbits introduced to Australia

In 1859 Thomas Austin, an English tenant farmer made good, introduced 24 wild rabbits to the Australian countryside. Austin, like others before him, dreamed of recreating English pursuits and even fauna in the alien surroundings of Australia. Attempts were made to introduce both rabbits and foxes so that they could be hunted in the traditional fashion. Prior to Austin, the attempts had failed, but at Austin's farm in Geelong, Victoria, the rabbits flourished and before long Australia was subject to one of the greatest population explosions of an introduced species in history.

At first the rabbit explosion seemed like a boon. Hunters boasted of shooting 1,200 rabbits in three hours. New industries were created: rabbit meat canning and rabbit fur felting for hats. But within 30 years Austin's dream had turned into Australia's nightmare. Rabbits were destroying crops and laying waste to natural habitats, particularly the pasture land farmers needed for sheep and cattle. In 1888, the Intercolonial Royal Commission on Rabbit Destruction offered a large reward for a biological control agent to reduce rabbit populations, but it went unclaimed.

In 1901 another Royal Commission came up with the idea of a physical barrier to stop the spread of rabbits, and thus was born the Rabbit-Proof Fence, which ran for 1,118 miles (1,800 km) across Australia. Despite widespread disagreement over its merits, the Fence lives on today, though it is now shorter (at just 727 miles, or 1170 km) and described as the Emu Fence, intended to stop large-scale emu migrations during droughts.

▼ By 1910, the rabbit population covered the best part of three-quarters of Australia.

27

Length of time spent in prison by Nelson Mandela (years)

Nelson Mandela was imprisoned from 1963 to 1990, 18 years of which he spent on Robben Island, a high-security prison for political prisoners, notorious for the brutality of its regime. Mandela's time in prison helped to form his politics, personality, and authority, and to transform him into a global symbol of defiance against injustice and oppression. His imprisonment marked the darkest chapter of the apartheid regime in South Africa, while his release signaled the beginning of its dismantling.

Mandela had been born into a royal family from the Transkei region of South Africa, renouncing his royal claims when he became a lawyer, but never losing his regal demeanor or authority. After helping found the radical Youth League of the moribund African National Congress in 1946, he organized protests and resistance against the increasingly oppressive and racist apartheid laws introduced from 1948. Mandela was arrested and imprisoned in the 1950s, and forced to operate clandestinely as one of the ANC's leaders. In 1960 the Sharpeville massacre, in which police fired on a crowd of unarmed anti-apartheid demonstrators and killed 72 of them, finally convinced him that the apartheid regime could only be countered by armed resistance.

After training abroad, Mandela returned to South Africa in July 1962 and was soon arrested. Not long after, the ANC's secret headquarters at Rivonia farm were raided and Mandela and seven others were put on trial for sabotage, conspiracy to overthrow the government, and assisting armed invasion. Mandela gave a famous speech at the trial, declaring "I cherish the ideal of a democratic and free society in which all persons live together in harmony and with equal opportunities. It is an ideal I hope to live for and to achieve. But if needs be, it is an ideal for which I am prepared to die."

The Rivonia Eight were sentenced to life imprisonment on Robben Island, notorious for its lime quarry where prisoners were forced to do hard labor. Mandela arrived in the winter of 1964 and for the next 18 years his home was a small cell, in which he had to sleep on the floor, use a bucket for a toilet, and break rocks in the quarry (although his conditions improved slightly after 1978). Inmates were allowed to exchange a single letter every six months and receive one visitor a year for just half an hour at a time.

▲ Mandela publicly burns his pass book on March 28th, 1960, shortly after the Sharpeville Massacre.

Emerging as the leader of the political prisoners, Mandela refused to be broken by his ordeal, bending the prison authorities to his will and even contriving to smuggle out his autobiography. He became an international cause célèbre, with a global campaign to secure his freedom. In 1982 he was transferred to a prison in Cape Town but refused to renounce violent action to secure his release. In 1988, the year he turned seventy, Mandela was moved to a prison hospital and then to a cottage, while engaging in negotiations with the government of new South African president F. W. De Klerk. Finally, in 1990, he was released, to national and international rejoicing. In 1993 he shared the Nobel Peace Prize with De Klerk, and in 1994 he was elected president of free, majority-ruled South Africa, serving until 1999. He died in 2013.

30

The Thirty Years' War

The Thirty Years' War was a terrible series of conflicts over religion and dynastic ambitions, which devastated Germany and cost the lives of 8 million people. More properly seen as a series of wars, the conflict initially flared up as the result of attempts by the Hapsburg Emperor to impose Catholic observance on Protestant realms in his domains, but grew to encompass a wider geopolitical struggle for European dominance between the Bourbons of France and the Hapsburgs of Spain and Austria. As the war dragged on, it was characterized by the depredations of roving armies seeking supplies and booty, with widespread pillage and rape. European powers from Britain and Sweden to Spain and the Ottoman Empire were dragged into the conflict, with battles raging as far afield as Brazil and Sri Lanka.

The defenestration of Prague

In the early 17th century Germany did not exist; instead a patchwork of around a thousand territories and states, divided between Catholic and Protestant faiths, made up the Holy Roman Empire. Ferdinand II of Styria was a scion of the powerful Hapsburg Dynasty, which exercised loose suzerainty over the Empire, controlling some territories directly. Bohemia was one of these; it held the casting vote among the seven electors who chose the Holy Roman Emperor. The other six were divided evenly between Protestant and Catholic. Bohemia was Protestant, its religious privileges supposedly safeguarded despite the Catholic faith of the ruling Hapsburgs. Ferdinand began to curtail those privileges, provoking the Bohemians to revolt. On May 23rd, 1618, two Catholic governors sent by Ferdinand were thrown out of a second-story window at Hradschin Castle, falling 50 feet (15 m) before landing, according to tradition, on a dung heap, although they survived. This symbolic rejection of Hapsburg authority, known as the Defenestration of Prague, is said to mark the start of the Thirty Years' War. Protestant Bohemia now rebelled and drove out Imperial (i.e. Ferdinand's) forces, deposing Ferdinand and awarding the Bohemian crown to a brash young Protestant prince, Frederick V of the Rhineland Palatinate, son-in-law of James I of England. He only survived as king for the winter of 1619–20, and so is known as the Winter King.

Ferdinand put together a coalition between Austria, Spain, Protestant Saxony, and the German Catholic League led by Bavaria, and his forces crushed the Bohemians at the Battle of White Mountain in November 1620. In 1622 the armies of the Catholic League, led by Baron von Tilly, conquered the Palatinate, forcing Frederick into exile in Holland. Protestantism in Bohemia was brutally extirpated and Counter-Reformational zeal spread to Austria and elsewhere. This marked the end of the initial phase of the war.

Battles continued, however, with the Bavarians chasing Protestant armies through northern Germany and a terrible new force under the mercenary general Albrecht von Wallenstein wreaking havoc on Protestant populations. Christian IV, king of Denmark and duke of Holstein, now saw a chance to set himself up as leader of the Protestant cause, but failed to attract the support he needed, and between 1625 and 1629 the "Danish phase" of the war

▼ Protestant majority areas and Hapsburg lands at the outset of the Thirty Years' War.

Protestant Majority

Hapsburg Rule

resulted in a string of defeats for the Protestants. Tilly and Wallenstein seemed unstoppable, overrunning northern Germany and most of Denmark, and Ferdinand was now poised to assert Hapsburg hegemony. In 1629 he issued the Edict of Restitution, which sought to overturn the religious settlements of the previous century, claw back the territories of Protestant princes, and eliminate Protestantism from the Empire.

This, however, was a step too far, and now the war changed from a primarily religious tussle within Germany to a wider conflict over the balance of power within Europe. Ferdinand's success threatened to create a Hapsburg domination of Europe, with powerful kingdoms in Spain, Austria, Germany, and the Spanish Netherlands, to the alarm of Bourbon France, which feared being encircled. Catholic France now allied with the Protestant Swedish king Gustavus Adolphus, and his invasion of Pomerania in July 1630 ultimately saved Protestant Germany.

▼ The Swedish king Gustavus Adolphus at Breitenfeld, one of his greatest victories.

Gustavus Adolphus was a brilliant commander with a disciplined army, funded by subsidies from France. In September 1631 he achieved a stunning victory over Tilly's imperial forces at Breitenfeld. Earlier that year the imperial capture of Magdeburg had unleashed one of the grimmest atrocities of the war, when the city was sacked by troops under Count Gottfried Pappenheim, who massacred every man, woman, and child (25,000 in all) and razed every building but the cathedral. Gustavus Adolphus was killed during the Swedish victory at Lützen the following year, having accounted for Tilly and Pappenheim, but Swedish forces continued to make a nuisance of themselves for many more years.

War as hell

Wallenstein was now left as the leading general for the imperial faction, but he was essentially a mercenary and unpopular with many on his own side. When removed from command he was already trying to sell his services to the other side; in 1634 he was assassinated by an Irish mercenary. That same year Swedish forces were defeated at Nördlingen, and in 1635 a partial peace between many German states brought to an end the Swedish phase of the war. The fourth and final phase, known as the French-Swedish, or general phase, ground on for 13 more years. Armies roamed the land, rarely meeting in decisive battles, seeking to monopolize resources. Areas such as Pomerania, Bohemia, and the Black Forest lost half of their populations. Agriculture and commerce were shattered across Germany.

French and Swedish victories, at Rocroi (1643) and Jankau (1645) respectively, and the death of Ferdinand II in 1637, drove the Hapsburgs to sue for peace. After five years of negotiation, the Treaties of Westphalia were signed in 1648. The religious liberty of the German princes was recognized, along with the integrity and autonomy of their states. The war itself had seen the transition from religion as the cause of war to geopolitics and reasons of state, and the removal of religion from the arena of European power politics was one of the primary consequences of this ruinous conflict.

33

The year Jesus was crucified

The date traditionally given for the crucifixion of Jesus Christ is Friday, April 3rd, in the year 33. In fact, while the day and even to some extent the date can be inferred from the Gospels, the year is very uncertain. The most precise guide given by the Gospels, and attested by a mention in the *Annals* of the Roman historian Tacitus, is that the crucifixion occurred while Pontius Pilate was procurator of Judaea, giving a date range of 26–36 CE.

The crucifixion itself is regarded as one of the two historically attested events of the life of Jesus, the historical figure (the other is his baptism by John the Baptist). Pinning down a precise chronology for the life of Jesus, however, has generated a vast industry of scholarship. He was probably born before 4 BCE, as the Gospels say his birth came just before the death of Herod the Great (37–4 BCE). His earthly father, Joseph, was a carpenter from Nazareth in Galilee, and Jesus is said to have trained as a carpenter himself. His ministry began after his baptism, around the age of 30, and although it lasted for only 1–3 years (the Gospels disagree), he generated enough of a following to alarm the Jewish authorities who governed Judaea, along with their Roman overlords. Accordingly he was tried, executed, and Christians believe resurrected, and later assumed into heaven.

The Christian Church that grew up around the figure and teachings of Christ and his followers (notably the Apostles and Paul) eventually grew to be the most widespread of world religions. Today there are around 2 billion Christians in the world.

40

Acres and a mule

The reparation offered to some freed black slaves during the American Civil War came to be known by the shorthand phrase "40 acres and a mule." This was based on Special Field Order 15, issued on January 16th, 1865, by General William Sherman from his base in Savannah, Georgia, not long after he had completed his famous "March to the Sea" campaign through the South.

Four days before issuing his order, Sherman and Secretary of War Edwin M. Stanton had met with local black leaders. "For the first time in the history of this nation," Stanton later reported, "the representatives of the government had gone to these poor debased people to ask them what they wanted for themselves." At the January 12th meeting, Sherman and Stanton met with 20 Baptist and Methodist ministers from the black community, nine of whom had formerly been slaves, and asked them about their future.

▲ William Tecumseh Sherman in May 1865, wearing a black armband to mark the recent death of President Lincoln.

"Each family shall have a plot"

Land redistribution to shatter the economic base of the Southern slaveholding class had previously been advocated by leading abolitionists. The black ministers consulted by Sherman were motivated by more immediate needs: "The way we can best take care of ourselves," pointed out the leader of the group, Reverend Garrison Frazier, "is to have land, and turn it and till it by our own labor... and we can soon maintain ourselves and have something to spare..." Asked "in what manner you would rather live, whether scattered among the whites, or in colonies by yourselves?" Frazier replied, presciently, "I would prefer to live by ourselves, for there is a prejudice against us in the South that will take years to get over." Most of the other ministers agreed with him.

Accordingly, having obtained the assent of President Lincoln, Sherman issued his famous order, detailing that a 400,000 acre strip of land including "The islands from Charleston, south, the abandoned rice fields along the rivers for thirty miles back from the sea, and the country bordering the St. Johns river, Florida, are reserved and set apart for the settlement of the negroes [sic] now made free by the acts of war and the proclamation of the President of the United States." Section 3 of the order specified, "each family shall have a plot of not more than forty acres of tillable ground." There was no mention of a mule, although the army was later able to lend some surplus mules to settlers who rushed to take up the offer.

▲ The approximate extent of the land reserved for redistribution by Sherman's Special Field Order 15.

When Christmas comes

Though limited in its scope, this dramatic land redistribution was a radical act. It gave rise to a widespread belief among the southern black community that "40 acres" would soon be enshrined as a universal right, with a huge land distribution expected to come in the near future (Christmas was widely touted as the date). But Lincoln's assassination and his replacement by Andrew Johnson, determined to rebuild the Union and achieve some sort of reconciliation with the South, meant that the "40 acres" promise would prove illusory. On May 29th, 1865, Johnson declared an amnesty to many Southerners, including the return of confiscated lands, and the land described in Sherman's Field Order would eventually revert back to its former owners.

In place of land redistribution, the solution promoted to the "problem" of the freed slaves was wage labor, under which blacks would be paid for their work but not allowed to own land themselves; this evolved into the sharecropping system, where tenant farmers worked land for its owners in return for a share of the produce. The inevitable result was that freed slaves struggled to build up and pass on capital. Black farmland ownership in the USA peaked at just 15 million acres in 1910 but then declined rapidly. By 1982, only 1.5 percent of the nation's farmers were black.

The price of slavery

What would have happened if the promise of the "40 acres" land redistribution had been carried through? At the time of the Civil War, there were around 4 million enslaved African Americans; assuming this equates to about a million families, meeting the "40 acres" promise would have meant redistributing 40 million acres—an area roughly the size of Georgia. This is sometimes dismissed as an impossibility, but in the 18th and 19th centuries land grants on a vast scale were not uncommon. The Donation Land Claim Act of 1850, for instance, offered homesteaders up to 640 acres (258 hectares) of free land in the Oregon Territory.

▲ A family on Smith's Plantation, Beaufort, South Carolina, in 1862. For a brief while in 1865 they might have believed they would be granted 40 acres.

The consequences for the economic history of African Americans are almost incalculable, although there have been efforts to put a figure on it. Martin Luther King, for instance, calculated that reparations for slavery based on the approximate value of 40 acres and a mule would total $800 billion (around $6.4 trillion in today's money). Could any amount of money compensate for the centuries of slavery inflicted on African Americans? In the 1990s, *Harper's* magazine calculated that between 1619 and 1865, African American slaves provided 222,505,049 hours of forced labor, and that the debt owed for this work, with compound interest, added up to $97 trillion. In fact, the only reparations made during the Civil War were to former slaveowners, who were paid $300 per freed slave.

42

Lines on a page

Johannes Gutenberg's Bible, known as the 42-Line Bible because most of the pages are printed with 42 lines, was the first printed book in Europe, or indeed anywhere outside of Eastern Asia. It was produced around 1453–55. An object of great beauty and technical sophistication, it announced the arrival of one of the greatest and most important inventions in history, printing with movable metal type, or as Gutenberg's contemporaries described it, "the art of multiplying books."

Movable type

Printing, the impression of marks on a medium, dates back to the earliest writing, cuneiform, which was made by pressing a wedge-shaped stylus into soft clay. Block printing was known in China from at least the 8th century CE, and the earliest known printed book, the *Diamond Sutra*, dates to 868 CE. In block printing each page is printed from a block that has been hand-carved specifically, which is slow and laborious. Movable type, which is where each character in a script is represented by a single, small block, or type, allows lines of type to be assembled to order, and then reordered for different texts, with much greater speed and efficiency. The first book printed by movable type, using type cast in bronze, was published in Korea in the late 14th century, but it was in the work of Gutenberg that the process would first be properly realized.

A marvelous man

Gutenberg was born to a patrician family in Mainz, in the Rhineland, around 1400. Entrepreneurial in spirit, around 1448 he borrowed a substantial sum of money, presumably to set up his printing workshop, where he would combine three innovations: a technique for rapid, precision casting of type; extremely dark, oil-based printer's ink sticky enough to stay on the type; and a press with which to apply the ink evenly to the page. Above all Gutenberg had the vision to combine these three elements into a unified process, achieving a remarkably complete technology that remained essentially unchanged into the 19th century.

Around 1453 Gutenberg and his partners, Johann Fust and Peter Schoeffer, started work on their edition of the Bible, eventually printing 180 copies. Each Bible comprised 1286 pages, with 42 lines of Latin text in fine Gothic type, with illuminations and colorful initial letters added by hand. Each page was printed using around 2,500 pieces of type, and Gutenberg had to cast 300 unique pieces of type. The book weighed 14 lb (6.35 kg), and probably sold for around 30 florins, three times a clerk's salary! In a letter of March 12th, 1455, Enea Silvio Piccolomini, later Pope Pius II, wrote that in Frankfurt a "marvelous man" had been promoting his copies of the Bible, printed so clearly that they could be read without glasses.

Although Gutenberg fell out with his partners and himself never produced a comparable volume, his printing press unleashed a revolution in human affairs, leading to a rapid rise in literacy in Europe and contributing directly to the Renaissance, the Scientific Revolution, and the Protestant Reformation.

▼ A Gutenberg Bible at the New York Public Library; when the first copy of the 42-line Bible arrived in New York, customs agents doffed their caps.

50

Percentage of Europeans killed by the Black Death

In 1347 a terrible disease arrived on the shores of Europe, capable of killing healthy men and women overnight, inflicting horrible suffering with painful swellings, blackening of the skin, vomiting, raving delirium, and bloody sputum. Infection spread from port to port, up rivers and along roads, moving around Europe like a wave. The poor records of the era make it hard to estimate the numbers killed, but death rates of between a third and half the population are accepted—possibly even more. The effects of this plague on the social, economic, and cultural order of medieval Europe were profound.

▲ A plague doctor, equipped with protective mask, complete with perfume-filled "beak" to guard against pestilential miasma.

The Universal Plague

The disease that later came to be called the Black Death was known to contemporaries as the Great Pestilence, the Great Mortality, and the Universal Plague. It probably arose in the steppes of Central Asia, spreading to China and India where it wreaked unknown havoc. Its arrival in Europe was the result, according to the Piacenzan chronicler, Gabriele de Mussis, of an early instance of biological warfare. In 1346, Genoese merchants at Caffa in the Crimea (present-day Feodosiya) were under siege by the "Tatars" (the Golden Horde of the Kipchak Khanate), when the Mongols were afflicted with a terrible plague. Forced to depart, the Tatars "ordered that their dead be loaded onto their catapults and lobbed into the city."

Fleeing the pestilential city, Genoese merchants sailed back to the Mediterranean and introduced the plague to Cyprus and Sicily in October 1347, and to Genoa in January 1348. By 1352 it had spread to Scandinavia and Russia (see map). The suffering and mortality it caused was shocking. All over Europe, Jews were blamed for spreading the pestilence, and vicious pogroms against them forced many to migrate to Eastern Europe.

Mainstream opinion points to the bacteria *Yersinia pestis* as the cause; today this organism still causes bubonic plague outbreaks, and is spread by disease-carrying fleas. But there are many dissenting voices, who point out that modern accounts of bubonic plague differ greatly from the medieval accounts, and that the epidemiology of the disease does not match up with rodent/flea transmission. The true nature of the Black Death remains mysterious, and there is also debate over its impact on the socio-economy of Europe.

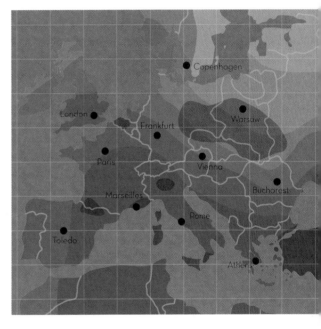

▼ The spread of the plague in Europe, showing that parts of Eastern Europe got off relatively lightly.

	1347
	mid-1348
	early 1349
	late 1349
	1350
	1351
	after 1351
	minor outbreak

The death of feudalism

The conventional view is that, by dramatically reducing the labor force, the Black Death revolutionized the relationship between peasants and landowners, driving up wages, living standards, and social status among the poorest. One result was that landowners switched to less labor-intensive agriculture, such as sheep-rearing, and in England, for instance, this led to a booming wool economy in the later Middle Ages. An alternative view is that the feudal system was already on the way out, and the Black Death merely expedited the transition. The cultural and religious ramifications of the plague were also profound in Europe, and have been linked to the Renaissance and the Reformation.

55

Dogs depicted on
the Bayeux Tapestry

The Bayeux Tapestry, which is actually a piece of embroidery, is a 224-foot (68-m) long, 20-inch (0.5-m) high linen cloth embroidered with as many as ten different colors of wool. The colors were made by combining three vegetable dyes: madder for reds, dyer's rocket for yellow, and indigo (made from woad) for blues and greens. It shows the story of William of Normandy's conquest of England, from the reign of King Edward the Confessor in 1064, to the Battle of Hastings in 1066. It weighs 771 lb (350 kg).

The narrative is shown in a central band, roughly 13 inches (33 cm) high, with upper and lower borders of about 2.75 inches (7 cm) showing animals, fanciful creatures, and even episodes from Aesop's Fables. In all, the Tapestry depicts 1,512 objects, including 623 people, 202 horses and mules, 55 dogs, 505 other animals (including mythical ones), 37 buildings, 41 ships and boats, and 49 trees. One of the most famous elements, an arrow that has been shot into the eye of a figure supposed to be the English King Harold, was probably added later, by mistake. Where and for whom the Tapestry was made is uncertain. Its historical accuracy and stylistic clues suggest it was made not long after 1066, and some believe it to have been commissioned by Odo, Bishop of Bayeux, half-brother of William the Conqueror. But a 1430 reference to what sounds very much like the Tapestry has been found in records from the Court of Burgundy, so perhaps the association with Bayeux is wrong. One influential alternative theory is that the Tapestry was made in Canterbury, in England.

56

Signatories to the
Declaration of Independence

On June 7th, 1776, at the Second Continental Congress, a committee was appointed to draft a formal declaration of independence of the 13 colonies from Britain. Thomas Jefferson, a lawyer from Virginia, was set to draft it. On July 4th Congress officially adopted the final text of the Declaration of Independence. However, it was not signed at this time, as the high-quality, durable document necessary had not yet been created. The text would have to be "engrossed"—written out in a clear hand on specially prepared vellum.

In the meantime, the "Committee of Five" (Thomas Jefferson, John Adams, Benjamin Franklin, Roger Sherman, and Robert R. Livingston) were given the job of having the text set and printed so that it could be distributed across the colonies. That very evening, Philadelphia printer John Dunlap ran off hundreds of copies. Only 26 of these "Dunlap Broadsides" survive.

It was not until August 2nd that John Hancock, President of the Congress, signed his name with a flourish, followed by 50 others. A further five delegates signed later. The signatories were drawn from all 13 colonies; 48 of them were native-born Americans, but eight had been born in Britain or Ireland. The youngest, Edward Rutledge, was just 26 years old, while Benjamin Franklin was the oldest at 70. Two of the signatories, John Adams and Thomas Jefferson, would go on to become the second and third presidents of the newly independent United States of America, and both men passed away on the 40th anniversary of the Declaration.

▼ Thomas Jefferson, Benjamin Franklin, and John Adams meet at Jefferson's lodgings in Philadelphia to review a draft of the Declaration of Independence.

60

Percentage of casualties
on Western Front
caused by shellfire

By the end of November 1914, just four months after the outbreak of World War I, the Western Front stretched 440 miles (700 km) from the Swiss-French border to the North Sea in an unbroken line of trenches. This was not the war Germany had planned for. Since 1905 the German general staff had developed a grand strategy, the Schlieffen Plan, which envisaged their armies wheeling through Belgium and Luxembourg to outflank French defensive lines, before capturing Paris and taking France out of the war. This plan fell apart when the German advance was turned back at the Battle of the Marne (September 5th–9th), but the Germans in turn halted the Allied counter-attack at the Battle of the Aisne (September 12th–28th), where entrenched positions made it impossible for either side to prevail.

The Race to the Sea

Now the war turned into a "Race to the Sea," in which each side tried to outflank the other's lines, with the point of attack shifting steadily northwest. A string of battles followed: Picardy, Albert, Arras, La Bassée, Messines, Armentières, Yser, Ypres, Langemarc, Gheluvelt, and Nonneboschen. By the time the battles at Ypres and Nonneboschen were over on November 22nd, the line of trenches had reached the North Sea near Nieuport. Before long the other end of the Western Front had reached the border between France and neutral Switzerland at the village of

Exterior

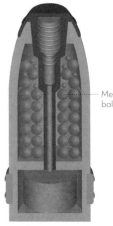

Metal balls

Cross-section

▲ Section through a shrapnel shell, filled with metal balls; this is the 20th-century version of grapeshot.

Pfetterhouse. Astonishingly, this marked the end of mobile warfare until 1917. A photograph of July 1917 shows the extreme northwestern end of the Western Front, with the massive system of trenches bisecting Western Europe ending in a small bunker overlooking the beach and the North Sea.

Trench warfare

Most of the rest of the war on the Western Front descended into the miasma of trench warfare, where the average life expectancy of a soldier was just six weeks—less for junior officers and stretcher bearers, the people most at risk. Although it is the machine gun, the bayonet, and poison gas that most vividly inhabit the historical imagination of trench warfare, the major sources of casualties were actually shellfire and disease. The latter accounted for a third of deaths in the Great War, and very widespread illness, from trench foot and dysentery caused by trench life, to the 150,000 British soldiers with venereal diseases, partly thanks to semi-official brothels set up behind the front lines.

At least 60 percent of casualties on the Western Front came from the effects of shells, mortars, and the like. The psychological effects of the relentless bombardment, and the intensity of combat in general, led to recognition of what was thought to be a new phenomenon: shell shock. At least 80,000 cases were recorded, although the actual total was probably much higher. In fact, cases of what is now called acute or post-traumatic stress disorder were known from earlier conflicts (it was called "nostalgia" in the American Civil War, for instance).

▼ British gunners at the front in 1914, loading shells into a gun protected from aerial observation by thatch.

60

Oxen required to
move the Basilica

Basilica was the name given to a colossal bombard—a cast bronze tube used as a cannon—which was the largest gun ever made at the time and helped the Ottoman sultan Mehmed II to take Constantinople. For over a thousand years, the great walls of the city had proven impregnable, enabling Constantinople to withstand 23 sieges by groups as diverse as the Avars, Rus, Bulgars, and Arabs. Numerous attempts by Muslim powers to take the city had failed, and by the mid-15th century the city was all that survived of the Byzantine empire, all of Asia Minor (now Turkey) and much of the Balkans having been overrun by the Ottomans.

To shatter the walls of Babylon

In 1452 a Hungarian cannon-maker named Orban offered his services to Constantine XI, the last emperor of Byzantium, but the destitute ruler was unable to pay him. Instead Orban went to Mehmed, who was planning an assault on the great city, and told him, "I can cast a cannon of bronze with the capacity of the stone you want. I have examined the walls of the city in great detail. I can shatter to dust not only these walls with the stones from my gun, but the very walls of Babylon itself."

That fall Orban set to work casting a monstrous bombard, which the Greeks would name the Basilica—"the royal gun." It was 27 feet (8.2 m) long, with walls of solid bronze 8 inches (20 cm) thick and a bore diameter of 30 inches (76 cm), so that a man could crawl inside. It could hurl a stone shot weighing around 1500 lb (725 kg) over a distance of a mile, but took so long to reload and set up that it would only be able to fire seven times a day.

Bears and cubs

The bombard was so heavy it required a team of 60 oxen to haul it and 200 men to handle it and prepare a site. But the great heat and violence of the explosions within were more than the metallurgy of the day could handle. When the siege started in April 1453, the Basilica would fire just a few times before it fell apart, but it inflicted great terror on the beleaguered inhabitants of Constantinople, and the Sultan had 68 other cannons, many of them monsters in their own right. Each large cannon was supported by a group of smaller ones to form a battery nicknamed "the bear with its cubs." The bears and cubs kept up a constant bombardment, so that by May 28th, after 47 days of relentless pounding, the Ottomans had blown up 55,000 lb (25 tonnes) of gunpowder and hurled 5,000 shots, breaching the walls that had withstood a millennium of assault. The age of artillery had rendered medieval castle fortifications obsolete. On May 29th Mehmed ordered a full frontal assault and the great city finally fell. One of the few surviving defenders later recalled that, as the Ottoman army descended on the shattered walls amid the roar of cannon fire, "the very air seemed to split apart... It seemed like something from another world."

▲ Mehmed II at the gates of Constantinople; his artillery breached defenses that had held for a millennium.

63

Clauses in the Magna Carta

In 1215, in a meadow at Runnymede, on the banks of the Thames, King John of England was forced by a group of angry barons to put his seal to a document listing their grievances and demands and promising redress to them. These Articles of the Barons had been negotiated over five days, and on June 15th the engrossed charter was sealed and issued. At this time it was known as the Charter of Runnymede, and within just 10 weeks John repudiated it, having had it annulled by the Pope. England was plunged into civil war and John died just over a year later. In 1217 the charter was reissued in the name of his infant son Henry III, after which it became known as Magna Carta.

The original Charter of Runnymede contained 63 clauses, although in the document the clauses are not numbered and the text reads continuously. Some of the clauses did not survive the 1217 reissue, but others are still enshrined in law today. Most of the clauses deal with grievances specific to medieval, feudal society, but the overall gist of the charter was that the King was not above the law of the land, must abide by that law and allow justice for all. The two most celebrated clauses, 39 and 40, state that "No free man shall be seized or imprisoned... except by the lawful judgment of his equals or by the law of the land," and that "To no one will we sell, to no one deny or delay right or justice." From these clauses derive the principles of *habeus corpus* (accused people are not to be held indefinitely without trial), trial by jury, and the presumption of innocence until proven guilty.

72

Length of the Chinese Imperial civil service exam (hours)

The examination system for the Chinese civil service was one of the most important and enduring elements of Chinese imperial civilization. It lasted for at least 1300 years, having been formalized at the very start of the 7th century CE and finally abolished in 1905. The core of the examination tested familiarity with classic texts of Confucianism, the philosophical and ethical system underpinning Chinese society for most of the Common Era.

Candidates were expected to demonstrate extensive knowledge of nine key works: the Four Books and the Five Classics. The Four Books were *The Analects*, *Mencius*, *Great Learning*, and *The Doctrine of the Mean*, while the Five Classics are the *Classic of Poetry*, the *Classic of History*, the *Classic of Rites*, the *Classic of Changes*, and the *Classic of Spring and Fall Annals*. The exams were extremely tough: in the 14th century, candidates were confined to bare cells for 24 hours for lower-level examinations and 72 hours for the top-level exams.

The rewards for those who succeeded could be significant, and competition was fierce. During the Ming Dynasty, for instance, only 1 in 6,000 candidates would earn a government position. The exam system gave the Emperor the means to break the power of the northern aristocracy, introducing in their place a meritocracy of powerful scholar-elite officials, who would owe their loyalty to the imperial system itself. It is said that when the emperor Li Shimin saw students coming into the exam court, he said excitedly, "All the heroes under the sky are in my pocket!"

▼ Scene from an examination during the Song Dynasty, when the civil service exam system became much more prominent, as bureaucrats displaced warrior-aristocrats from the elite.

80

The Eighty Years' War

The Eighty Years' War, also known as the Dutch Revolt and the Hapsburg–Dutch War, did not go on for 80 years according to most accounts. Its conventional start and end dates are 1566 and 1648, giving a span of 82 years, while open warfare raged between 1572 and 1609, and then again from 1621 to 1648.

The causes of the war were the religious and economic impositions made by the Hapsburg king of Spain, Philip II, on his Burgundian inheritance in the Low Countries. Under his father, Charles V, the 17 provinces of the Low Countries had been allowed considerable autonomy, particularly economically and religiously. Mercantile and commercial towns thrived while Protestantism spread through the provinces, especially the northern ones. When Philip came to the throne he wanted to increase taxation on the Low Countries and roll back the Protestant advances. He more than quadrupled the number of bishops there and unleashed the Inquisition, while also placing the administration of the Low Countries under his direct control. When 200 nobles protested in Brussels in 1566, they were derided as "beggars." Trouble flared: Catholic churches were burned and bread riots broke out. In 1567 Philip sent the Duke of Alba and 10,000 battle-hardened Spanish troops to stamp out the rebellion. This failed to subdue the northern provinces, and in 1572 the 17 provinces declared open rebellion, with William I "the Silent" of Nassau, aka the Prince of Orange, leading the resistance. A Dutch fleet of "sea beggars" seized important ports.

The Spanish fury

Although the Spanish had military superiority, Philip was unable to fully stamp out the Dutch rebellion. Conflicts with France, England, and the Ottomans constantly diverted his attention, and more seriously he was beset by constant cashflow crises. His 70–90,000-strong army in Flanders cost 30,000 ducats a day to maintain, and when they were not paid they were liable to mutiny, which they did 46 times between 1572 and 1607.

Eventually the provinces split along religious lines. The seven northern provinces formed the Union of Utrecht in 1579, and declared their independence as the United Provinces (aka the Dutch Republic) in 1581. The failure of Philip's Armada adventure against England in 1588 further weakened his hand, and war dragged on until 1609, when the exhausted parties signed the Twelve-year Truce. By this time Philip II and William I had been succeeded by Philip III and Prince Maurice.

The Dutch used the breathing space to build a mercantile and maritime empire, and when war resumed in 1621 they used their naval strength to wrest from the Spanish and their Portuguese vassals vital ports and trade concessions around the globe. The relentless assault of the Spanish had helped to make the Dutch into a global power, even as it helped bankrupt and tip Spain into terminal decline. Their mutual anxiety over the rising power of Bourbon France led the Spanish and Dutch to conclude the Treaty of Münster in 1648, recognizing the independence of the United Provinces.

▼ The starving and desperate inhabitants of Leiden, relieved in October 1574 after a brutal siege.

Fourscore and seven

The Gettysburg Address

Abraham Lincoln's famous speech was given on November 19th, 1863, at an event to dedicate part of the battlefield at Gettysburg to a cemetery where some of those who had fallen in the battle back in July could be properly interred. The Battle of Gettysburg was the greatest battle of the American Civil War and marked a turning point; it was the farthest northern limit of the advance of General Lee's Confederate Army, and after ill-advisedly attacking entrenched Union positions he had been beaten off with heavy losses and forced to retreat. Though it marked the beginning of the end for the Confederacy, it had hardly been an unalloyed triumph for the Union army, which had failed to press its advantage and, with 23,000 casualties, had been mauled almost as badly as the Confederates, with 25,000 casualties.

▲ Lincoln delivers his address at Gettysburg; the audience were surprised at its brevity.

A few appropriate remarks

It was in this context, of a shockingly bloody war entering its third year with no imminent end, that Lincoln had begun to consider a defining public statement of the purpose of the conflict. On November 2nd he was invited to contribute "a few appropriate remarks" to the forthcoming ceremony, and he started work on his speech while at the White House although he did not finish it until the night of November 18th, when he was staying at the home of David Wills, the man behind the cemetery project and the dedication.

Lincoln was not the main speaker; his remarks were prefaced by a two-hour-long oration by Edward Everett, a professor, politician, and statesman. When Lincoln gave his speech, the crowd was somewhat surprised to find that it lasted just two minutes. According to some accounts, the response of the 15,000-strong audience was muted and Lincoln himself is supposed to have muttered as he returned to his seat that it had been "a flat failure." Everett was in no doubt that he had seen something historic, writing to the president the next day, "I should be glad if I could flatter myself that I came as near the central idea of the occasion in two hours as you did in two minutes."

Lincoln's achievement was that in just 272 words he succeeded in recasting the purpose of not just the war but the nation itself. The war was not simply an attempt to restore the union, but a battle to preserve the fundamental ideal articulated in the Declaration of Independence—that all men are created equal. The nation, he averred, would have a new birth of freedom, and "government of the people, by the people, for the people, shall not perish from the earth." This last phrase may have been derived from an 1830 speech in the Senate by Daniel Webster, in which he spoke of "government, made for the people, made by the people, and answerable to the people," echoed in an 1850 speech by Theodore Parker declaring that the "American idea" is "a government of all the people, by all the people, for all the people." The Address, with its Biblical power and phrasing, has been linked to what is known as the "civil religion" of America: a synthesis of the secular and sacred to produce a spiritual mission for the nation and its political system.

▲ A draft of the Address, in Lincoln's own handwriting.

90

Percentage of Native Americans killed by smallpox

Smallpox was a viral disease that has now been eradicated thanks to a global health program in the 20th century, with the last naturally occurring case diagnosed on October 26th, 1977. For thousands of years before this it wreaked terrible havoc, ranking as one of the most deadly diseases in history with a historical death toll estimated at around 500 million.

A herd disease

The origins of the disease are uncertain but evidence of pustular rash on the mummy of Ramses V (ca. 1145 BCE) suggests it has been around since at least the 2nd millennium BCE, and outbreaks have been linked to a number of mystery plagues in the ancient world, such as the Athenian Plague and the Antonine Plague. Smallpox is an example of a "herd disease"; one which originates in large, dense animal populations but is able to make the jump to similar human populations thanks to close proximity between humans and domesticated animals. In the Old World, humans domesticated many species of animal, often living under the same roof as their herds, and milking and eating them. The constant exposure to smallpox meant that Old World populations developed some degree of immunity to it, although the death rate for those infected nonetheless remained at least 30 percent.

In the New World the only large animal domesticated was the llama, which was neither eaten nor milked, and was kept away from large human populations. Accordingly, New World natives had no exposure to herd diseases such as smallpox, and had not developed any degree of immunity. When explorers from the Old World arrived in the New from 1492 onward, the effect of the diseases they brought with them was devastating.

Piled with corpses

The first outbreak of smallpox in the New World occurred in 1495 in San Domingo on Hispaniola, killing around 80 percent of the natives. This was a harbinger of things to come, for smallpox and similar herd diseases turned out to be by far the most potent weapon of the conquistadors and colonizers. For instance, when Hernán Cortés attacked Tenochtitlan, capital of the Aztecs, in 1521, the city had already been devastated by a smallpox epidemic. Contemporary chronicler Bernal Díaz recorded that, when the Spanish entered the city, "We could not walk without treading on the bodies and heads of dead Indians. The dry land was piled with corpses."

▼ Conquistador Hernán Cortés, whose stunning triumph over the Aztecs was partly due to the devastation wreaked on them by smallpox.

Herd diseases swept across the New World, and are believed to have killed up to 90 percent of the indigenous populations, laying waste to advanced and populous civilizations, changing the course of history. Smallpox may have literally changed the planet, for there is increasing evidence from archaeological finds that, prior to European contact, the Amazon basin supported large populations and was extensively cultivated, raising the possibility that the Amazon rain forest itself is at least partly the result of the mass extermination of indigenous populations by smallpox, leaving vast tracts of farmland to be reclaimed by the jungle.

95

Theses of Martin Luther

On October 31st, 1517, Martin Luther posted a copy of a document he had written on the door of the Wittenberg Castle church. The *Disputation on the Power and Efficacy of Indulgences*, more popularly known as the Ninety-Five Theses, was a list of talking points for an academic theological debate he hoped to provoke. What he unleashed was the Reformation, a profound revolution in the religious, cultural, and geopolitical dispensation of Europe. The posting of the Ninety-Five Theses is traditionally given as the starting point for the Protestant Reformation.

Luther was a monk and theologian from Saxony whose research had convinced him that Scripture alone is the source of evangelical truth, and that salvation comes from faith alone, and not from earthly deeds. He particularly objected to the selling of indulgences, where relief from purgatory could be bought, and the arrival in Saxony of a cleric selling indulgences to pay for the renovation of St. Peter's in Rome led him to draw up his Theses.

In the Theses, Luther reserved harsh language for "those who preach indulgences," pointing out that "There is no divine authority for preaching that the soul flies out of purgatory immediately the money clinks in the bottom of the chest," and challenging the pope to renovate St. Peter's "with his own money rather than with the money of poor believers." Not surprisingly Luther landed in hot water with the Catholic Church, but when confronted at the Diet of Worms in 1521 he famously insisted he would not recant: "Here I stand. God help me. I can do no other."

▲ Legend has it that inspiration struck while Luther was on the toilet, and archaeological investigations have shown that his toilet was well appointed for philosophical pondering, equipped as it was with underfloor heating.

95

Synagogues burned in Vienna

Kristallnacht ("Crystal Night") was the name given to a massive outbreak of violence against Jewish people, synagogues, and property on the night of November 9-10th, 1938, also known as the Night of Broken Glass. The pretext for the pogrom was the shooting of a German diplomat in Paris; when news of it reached Adolf Hitler, he and Joseph Goebbels decided it was the perfect excuse to act against German Jewry. Storm troopers and paramilitaries around Germany (including Austria) were ordered to stage violent reprisals, under the guise of "spontaneous demonstrations." Just before midnight on November 9th, Heinrich Müller, chief of the Gestapo, sent a telegram to all police stations: "Actions against Jews and especially their synagogues will take place in all of Germany. These are not to be interfered with." Police were instructed to arrest Jewish victims, and fire crews to let synagogues blaze.

As a result of the pogrom at least 91 Jews were killed and more than 1,000 synagogues were burned or damaged, along with 7,500 Jewish-owned businesses, and hospitals, schools, homes, and cemeteries were also vandalized. Jews were forced to clean up the mess themselves, and any insurance compensation was confiscated, while a massive collective fine was levied on the Jewish community. Around 30,000 Jewish men were arrested and sent to concentration camps. *Kristallnacht* signaled the final destruction of any illusions that German Jews still held about the possibility of life under the Nazis.

100

The Hundred Years' War

The Hundred Years' War was a series of conflicts between England and France conventionally dated as running between 1337 and 1453. The roots of the conflict lay in tension between the thrones over the territory of Aquitaine, English influence in Flanders, and French influence in Scotland. Through the maternal line Edward III of England had a claim to the French throne. In 1337 Philip VI of France declared Edward's lands in France forfeit in retaliation for an embargo on wool trade with Flanders, and Edward invaded. Although France was far larger and more powerful than England, the English developed battle tactics based around yeomen archers that won them great victories, the first coming at Crécy in 1346, after which Edward took Calais in 1347. His son, Edward of Woodstock, the Black Prince, won another great victory at Poitiers in 1356, capturing the French king.

▼ Manuscript illustration showing the Battle of Crécy in 1346.

The Treaty of Troyes

In the 1370s, alliance with the kingdom of Castile brought the French king Charles V naval supremacy, allowing him to defeat an English fleet at La Rochelle in 1372. A truce signed in 1396 lasted until 1415, when the new king of England, Henry V, renewed the conflict and won an overwhelming victory at Agincourt (see page 32), going on to conquer Normandy and securing the Treaty of Troyes (1420), in which Charles VI agreed to disown his son, the Dauphin, and recognize Henry, who now controlled Paris and all of northern France, as his heir. This marked the high point of English gains in France.

▲ Joan of Arc, the Maid of Orleans, shown in an illustration from the late 15th century.

Joan of Arc

In 1422 both kings died and the boy king Henry VI became the only English king to be crowned King of France in France. The Dauphin refused to recognize him, and with the inspiration of Joan of Arc, the Maid of Orleans, a farmer's daughter motivated by voices in her head, his forces started to drive back the English. In 1429 Joan lifted the siege of Orleans and stood beside the Dauphin as he was crowned Charles VII at Reims. She was captured by the Burgundians and turned over to their allies, the English, to be burned as a heretic in 1431. Charles, who had not intervened on her behalf, concluded a treaty with the Burgundians, uniting France, and took Paris in 1436.

By 1450 the French had regained control of Normandy, and the following year they conquered Aquitaine and Bordeaux, which had been an English possession for three hundred years. An expeditionary force of 1452 under John Talbot, Earl of Shrewsbury, recovered some of Gascony, but the following year Talbot was killed at Castillon and Bordeaux surrendered. The Hundred Years' War was over and only Calais remained as the last English foothold in France. The next time an English army landed in France, in 1475, Louis XI bought off the invasion, and Calais finally fell in 1558. The long war had despoiled much of France and may have reduced the country's population by as much as half.

100

Duration of Napoleon's restoration (days)

On March 20th, 1815, Napoleon arrived in Paris to complete one of history's greatest comebacks. A hundred days later he would be gone for good, and what the French came to call *les Cent Jours* brought to a climax the convulsions and conflict of the Napoleonic era.

After his defeat at Leipzig in 1813, Napoleon had been forced to retreat into France as Allied armies pressed in relentlessly. Defeat was inevitable and in April 1814 Napoleon abdicated and went into exile on the Mediterranean island of Elba, near Corsica. Here he ruled a little kingdom and even had a 1,500-strong little army. Meanwhile, in Paris, the Bourbon monarchy was restored under Louis XVIII, and in Vienna the Great Powers of Europe met in congress to determine a new dispensation for Europe, intended to look very much like the old, pre-Revolutionary one.

By March 1815, Napoleon, still only 45 years old, had had enough of retirement and determined to take advantage of unrest over the Bourbon Restoration and the machinations at Vienna. On March 1st he landed with his little army at Cannes and began to march north, gathering support as he went. At Grenoble on March 7th, the government forces sent to oppose him defected to his side, and on March 13th Louis fled Paris for exile in Ghent. A week later Napoleon arrived in the capital, and was restored to power on the basis of concessions to liberal constitutionalists, which he soon discarded. He set about mobilizing new armies for the inevitable onslaught from the Quadruple Alliance (Britain,

▲ Jacques-Louis David's 1812 portrait of Napoleon in his study, which prompted the emperor to declare: "You have understood me, my dear David."

Prussia, Austria, and Russia), but political problems quickly eroded popular enthusiasm for his restoration, which would prove to have disastrous consequences on the morale of his troops.

At the Congress of Vienna the participants immediately agreed to remobilize their forces, each committing 180,000 men. Facing a coalition of almost every nation in Europe, Napoleon knew he had to strike quickly, concentrating his forces against individual enemies before they had a chance to combine. In June he marched into Belgium with 128,000 men and 358 guns, and although he was able to force back the Prussians at Ligny (June 16th), he was unable to break the line of the Duke of Wellington's Anglo-Allied army at Waterloo on June 18th. At the end of the day the Prussians, under Marshal Blücher, joined the fray, and the brittle French army abruptly collapsed. Napoleon fled to Paris but abdicated for a second time on June 22nd, leaving Paris on June 29th, 123 days after he had first left Elba. He surrendered to the British at La Rochelle on July 3rd after an abortive attempt to flee to America. This time the Allies made sure he would not return from exile, shipping him off to St. Helena, a lonely outpost in the middle of the South Atlantic where he would remain until his death on May 5th, 1821. The Allies took Paris on July 7th, restoring Louis XVIII to the throne the following day. The phrase "Hundred Days" was first used in a speech of welcome for him, to denote the approximate duration of his absence from Paris.

▲ Napoleon bids farewell to the Imperial Guard in the courtyard of the Palace of Fontainebleau.

125

Electoral democracies

According to the *Freedom in the World* survey carried out by Freedom House, in 2015, 125 of the world's 195 countries are electoral democracies, and 89 of those are liberal democracies with free citizens. This means that 46 percent of countries in the world, accounting for 40 percent of the world's population, are free, liberal democracies, and that the majority of countries have electoral democracies.

The end of history

According to the influential and popular theory of the American sociologist and political scientist Francis Fukuyama, as described in his 1992 bestseller *The End of History and the Last Man*, statistics like these show that history has reached some sort of climax. Fukuyama's contention is that human societies follow a kind of ideological/political evolution, and that the end point of that evolution is the form of government that is most stable: the liberal, capitalist democracy. His thesis was developed in the wake of the collapse of Communism in Russia and Eastern Europe, which saw one of the main alternative systems of government—socialism—give way to liberal democracies across the whole Eastern bloc. Accordingly Fukuyama suggested that liberal capitalist democracy was now the dominant form of government in the world and would inexorably become ubiquitous, so that history, when defined as the course of ideological/political evolution, was reaching its end point. He was at pains to point out that this did not mean the end of events, which is the more conventional view of history.

Fukuyama's argument was an elaboration of the theories of the Russian-French thinker Alexandre Kojève, who in turn was developing the historical perspective of German philosopher Georg Hegel. Hegel saw history as a progressive development producing social change; Kojève argued that this change revolved around the human desire for "recognition" and the drive to rectify inequalities in recognition. Authoritarian regimes are doomed to fail because they perpetuate these inequalities; liberal democracy and globalized capitalism make each person sovereign of their individual domain, and hence are the inevitable end point of the desire for recognition.

Defending the thesis

Fukuyama's thesis is controversial and has been critiqued on both practical and theoretical grounds. In particular it was argued in the wake of 9/11 that Fukuyama had jumped the gun, and not given sufficient attention to religious fundamentalism and its ideological and political challenge to liberal capitalist democracy. Fukuyama contended that terrorist attacks like these are "a series of rearguard actions." However, Freedom House points out that "the number of electoral democracies has not changed dramatically since the early 1990s." Writing in the *Oxford Companion to Politics of the World*, Fukuyama argues: "Human history, while progressive overall, has been full of wrong turns and retrogressions. At the end of the 20th century, however, one may question the likelihood of there being some obvious non-capitalist, non-liberal, non-democratic order that people simply haven't been imaginative enough to think up until now."

169

Conquistadors who conquered the Inca Empire

In 1532 Francisco Pizarro and a tiny Spanish force of just 106 foot soldiers and 62 horsemen conquered a mighty empire of hundreds of thousands, in one of the most audacious gambits in history, prompting Pizarro's secretary Francisco Xerez to wonder immodestly, "Whose deeds can be compared with those of Spain? Not even the ancient Greeks and Romans."

Pizarro had landed on the shores of the Inca Empire a year earlier and learned that it was riven by civil war between the brothers Huáscar and Atahualpa, vying for the title of *Sapa Inca* ("Sovereign Emperor"), vacated since the death of their father from smallpox. Atahualpa prevailed, and on November 16th, 1532, he brought his army of 80,000 to meet Pizarro at Cajamarca. In one of the most one-sided battles in history, the 169 conquistadors sprang a surprise attack on Atahualpa and his retinue, slaughtering up to 7,000 of them without losing a man. Atahualpa was captured and his baggage train and royal treasure looted. When he saw the conquistadors' lust for gold, Atahualpa tried to ransom himself by filling with gold the room in which he was being held prisoner, up to a height of 8 feet (2.45 m). The conquistadors greedily accepted the treasure, but murdered Atahualpa in July 1533.

▼ The Spanish seizing Atahualpa at Cajamarca; in reality the conquistadors hacked off the arms of his litter bearers to get at him.

297

Length of Phantom Time (years)

According to an extraordinary hypothesis developed by German researchers Heribert Illig and Hans-Ulrich Niemitz, the years 614–911 CE in the conventional chronology never really happened, and a large chunk of the early Middle Ages (often called the Dark Ages) was invented. In order to determine in which year you are reading this, subtract 297 from the year you think you are in.

This Phantom Time hypothesis (PTH) is based on apparent discrepancies in the dates of some medieval documents, and in the calendar reforms introduced by Pope Gregory XIII in 1582, in which ten days were removed from the old Julian calendar to correct for sloppy use of leap days. This ten-day shift corrects for errors accumulated over 1,257 years, yet the Julian calendar dates back to 45 BCE, leaving a discrepancy of more than three centuries. Coupled with apparent gaps in the historical record of early medieval Western Europe, and with the general cultural stasis that led to this period being known as the Dark Ages, this suggests to Phantom Time adherents that the period 614–911 CE is a forgery, inserted into the historical record around 980 CE by a conspiracy including the German emperor Otto II, partly in order to place his reign near the significant date of 1000 AD.

There are major flaws in the PTH, which is hopelessly Eurocentric. The apparent calendar discrepancy is easily explained by the fact that the Gregorian reforms were only intended to correct for discrepancies since 325 CE, the date of the Council of Nicaea.

▲ Pope Gregory XIII, whose reform of the calendar, to correct errors that had accumulated since the 4th century, confused the authors of the Phantom Time Hypothesis.

325

Year of the Council of Nicaea

The early Christian church had great diversity of doctrine, thanks to the high degree of autonomy of the various congregations. A particular source of controversy was the precise nature of Jesus Christ, in relation to God: Is Jesus of the same substance as God, or is there some degree of hierarchy between them? This was the basis of the Arian Controversy, named for the views of 4th-century Alexandrian priest Arius. It threatened to cause severe disorder in the Church, and in 324 the Roman emperor Constantine, who was less interested in zealous dogmatism than in imposing order, sought to limit the disturbance.

In an attempt to resolve the Controversy, Constantine convened a council of church leaders, the first such ecumenical ("from the whole world") council, meaning that it included ecclesiastical figures from the entire empire.

▲ Icon from the Eastern Orthodox tradition, depicting the First Council of Nicaea.

At Constantine's urging, the disputatious clerics agreed to ban Arius and adopt a creed, or statement of belief, acknowledging that Jesus and God are consubstantial. The Council of Nicaea subsequently became legendary in Christianity, and the central creed of Christianity was later known as the Nicene Creed, although in fact it differed from the creed adopted at Nicaea. The main significance of the Council of Nicaea is probably that it was the first in a long tradition of ecumenical church councils.

342

Chests of tea

The Boston Tea Party was a protest against British taxation in the Americas; it provoked a response that would in turn set America on the road to independence. The 1760s saw rising tension between the American colonies and the British government over issues such as governance and taxation. In 1768 the arrival in Boston of a large group of British soldiers, mainly Irish Catholics, steadily escalated the tension. Unruly behavior by both colonists and soldiers led to ugly incidents, culminating in the Boston Massacre of 1770, when a stone-throwing mob was fired upon. Of the eleven people hit, five subsequently died. The British sought to appease inflamed colonial sentiments by repealing many of the unpopular taxes, and tensions seemed to ease.

Tea time

American patriots, however, still chafed under the British yoke, and at least one of the hated taxes remained: the duty on tea imported by the colonies, which many Americans avoided by buying smuggled Dutch tea. This hit the revenues of the British East India Company (EIC), which was already in severe financial difficulties. Much of the British establishment had shares in the EIC, and in 1773 the British government passed the Tea Act, which would allow the EIC to sell tea in the American colonies without paying many of the usual taxes, and thus at a cheaper price than the smuggled Dutch tea. However, the tea would still be liable to a "per-pound" tax, and would be available only through a few, approved vendors. American patriots viewed this as a transparent conspiracy to make them accept imposed taxes while surrendering to a state-sanctioned monopoly; they were supported by angry merchants who faced being shut out of a lucrative market. Discontent peaked in Boston in late November, when ships bearing consignments of tea started to arrive.

Sons of Liberty

Mass meetings called for the resignation of the intended recipients of the tea, known as consignees, and when they demurred the protestors refused to allow the tea to be unloaded. They wanted the tea to be sent back to England, but were aware that if, within 20 days, the tea were not unloaded and the duty on it paid, it could be seized by customs officials, whereupon it would be handed to the consignees. A group of Boston radicals, the Sons of Liberty, led by Samuel Adams, determined that this must not be allowed to happen. On 16th December, the day before the tea was to be seized, another mass meeting of 5,000 citizens ended in calls for the tea to be dumped in the harbor. Over the next three hours 342 chests, containing over 90,000 lb (40 tonnes) of tea, worth £18,000, were dumped into the harbor. There was no violence or looting.

▼ A 19th-century imagining of the scene at the Tea Party, showing the Sons of Liberty in "Indian Dress," dumping tea into Boston Harbor.

The British response was to impose a series of restrictive and punitive acts, known in America as the Intolerable or Coercive Acts. These in turn riled American patriots and prompted the colonies to convene the first Continental Congress.

410

Year the Romans abandoned Britain

According to the traditional history of Britain, as still taught to schoolchildren, 410 CE is the date of the end of Roman Britain. In this year, the ancient scribe Zosimus wrote, the emperor Honorius "sent letters to the communities of Britain, bidding them defend themselves." The Roman legions had been withdrawn, and the emperor was making clear that no help would be forthcoming in the battle against ever-intensifying Germanic incursions. The province of Britain was cast adrift, abandoned by Rome to sink into the gloom of the Dark Ages.

In reality this view is overly simplistic, and the "Honorian Rescript," from an imperial edict issued by the beleaguered Roman emperor (who was shortly to see Rome sacked by the Visigoths), probably did not refer to Britain at all. All the other places mentioned in the edict are towns in Italy. By this time Roman armies were not organized into legions, and the "legions" supposedly withdrawn from Britain had been the militia of the imperial pretender Constantine III.

As central control of the empire waned in the early 5th century, territories such as Britain did indeed gain their "independence," but Britain did not slide into anarchy. Romano-British leaders retained much of Roman civilization, most notably the Latin language and Christian religion. Indeed, it appears the Anglo-Saxon "invasion" that followed was more of an integration with existing traditions, so that a line of cultural descent runs from early Romano-Britons to the Anglo-Saxon Alfred the Great.

600

Rooms in Pueblo Bonito

Pueblo Bonito is the largest of the Great Houses of the Ancestral Pueblo Peoples, popularly known as the Anasazi; American Indian communities that flourished around the years 920–1150 in what is now the Four Corners region of the U.S. Southwest. The Anasazi built a thriving community at Chaco Canyon in northern New Mexico, centered on large, multi-roomed complexes known as Great Houses, which were the largest buildings in pre-Columbian America, and remained the tallest in America until the first steel-girder skyscrapers went up in Chicago in the 1880s.

Anasazi means "ancient ones," and is the name given by the Navajo to peoples who formerly lived in southwest USA. Through their mastery of dry-land agriculture and development of extensive road and trade networks, the Anasazi were able to support a dense urban culture in an arid environment. Up to 10,000 people may have lived in Chaco Canyon at times, and they were capable of grand engineering projects such as Pueblo Bonito, which is up to six stories high and has more than 600 rooms. Over 200,000 huge logs were used to build the Canyon's pueblos, contributing to deforestation, which in turn led to the collapse of the Chaco Canyon culture.

▼ An imaginative 19th-century reconstruction of Pueblo Bonito in Chaco Canyon, New Mexico.

622

Year of the Hegira

The Hegira or *hijra*, from the Arabic word meaning "departure," "emigration," or "breaking off relations with," also known as the Exodus and the Flight to Medina, was the event that marked the start of the Islamic era and the Year 1 in the Islamic calendar. In 622 Mohammed, a former merchant of the Quraysh tribe, was preaching in Mecca. He had received divine revelations starting from 610, and had begun his mission to preach Islam from 613, but had made little headway in Mecca.

At this time Mecca, with its ancient shrine the Ka'aba, was the center of pagan worship in the Arabian peninsula, which meant that when Mohammed began preaching against idolatry and the polytheistic religion that supported it, few were receptive. But his message spread more successfully to the settlement of Yathrib, 200 miles (320 km) to the north, where he was able to establish a flourishing community of Muslims.

After learning that the Meccan authorities planned to assassinate him, in September 622 Mohammed and his companion Abu Bakr escaped and journeyed north to Yathrib. According to Islamic traditions, Mohammed's escape was facilitated by various divine interventions. Yathrib was later renamed Madinat al-Nabi, "the city of the Prophet," and eventually simply Medina, "the City." Here Mohammed established a power base from which in 630 he would return to Mecca as a conqueror, and the *hijra* has thus been used to mark the start of the Islamic calendar, with years denoted as AH, "Anno Hegirae."

673

Men in the Charge
of the Light Brigade

The Charge of the Light Brigade was a cavalry action that took place during the Battle of Balaclava on October 25th, 1854. It became infamous thanks to the suicidal bravery of the brigade, the tragic pointlessness of their sacrifice (occasioned by a misunderstood order), and the impact of contemporary reportage and subsequent immortalization in verse by Alfred Tennyson.

Battle for Balaclava

Balaclava was the entrepôt for supplies coming to the British expeditionary force laying siege to Sevastopol in the Crimea, and in 1854 it was the target of an advance by a Russian army under General Liprandi. Standing in the way of this force were the Heavy and Light Brigades of Lord Lucan's cavalry division, and the 93rd Highlanders infantry regiment, under the command of Lord Raglan. The battlefield consisted of parallel North and South Valleys, separated by a ridge called the Causeway Heights. The Russians quickly established positions at the eastern head and along both sides of the North Valley but were met by the Heavy Brigade and the Highlanders and driven back onto the Causeway Heights, where they started to remove guns they had captured. Raglan sent a famously vague order to Lucan telling him to "to advance rapidly to the front, and try to prevent the enemy carrying away the guns," but he did not specify which front, and thus were sown the seeds of a fatal miscommunication.

From his position at the western end of the North Valley, Lucan was unable to see the Russian activity on the Causeway Heights and asked which guns he should attack. Captain Lewis Nolan, the high-handed aide-de-camp who had been entrusted with delivering the message, insolently gestured vaguely east, declaring, "There is your enemy. There are your guns, My Lord." Stung by his manner, Lucan ordered Lord Cardigan, in charge of the 673 riders of the Light Brigade, to charge the Russian battery at the head of the North Valley. This entailed a suicidal charge along the bottom of a valley surrounded on three sides by enemy artillery. Although the Light Brigade managed to overrun their target, they were forced to retreat and once more run the gauntlet of Russian artillery.

By the time the action was over, 247 men had been killed or wounded and 475 horses lost. Nolan had been among the first to die, as he attempted to ride across the front of the charge to warn Cardigan of his mistake. The attack had been a complete failure, but the dauntless and unquestioning bravery of the Light Brigade struck a chord with Victorian Britain and their sacrifice was immortalized by the new Poet Laureate, Alfred Tennyson: "O the wild charge they made! All the world wondered. Honor the charge they made! Honor the Light Brigade, Noble six hundred!"

▲ The Light Brigade, led by Lord Cardigan, charges through the "Valley of Death," hammered by Russian batteries on three sides.

751

Year of the Battle of Talas

The Battle of Talas was the only time that Arab and Chinese armies clashed, on the banks of the Talas River in Central Asia. Defeat for the Chinese led indirectly to their withdrawal from the region, leaving it to be drawn, over the subsequent centuries, into the orbit of the Islamic Caliphate. Accordingly Talas is said to mark a turning point in history, determining the future course of a vast region of Central Asia with ramifications still felt today.

Transoxiana

Under the Tang, China had sought to expand its sphere of influence westward along the Silk Road, into the territories of the Tarim Basin and as far as the borders of Transoxiana, at the time one of the richest parts of Asia thanks to the flow of trade between East and West. Meanwhile the Islamic Caliphate, expanding eastward under the Ummayads, had also conquered territory as far as Transoxiana. In the space between them, client kingdoms jostled for position and survival.

In 750 the Caliphate was convulsed by a great rebellion, in which the Ummayads were overthrown and massacred by the Abbasids, whose power base lay in Khorasan in Persia. The center of gravity of the Caliphate abruptly shifted eastward, and the lands of Central Asia were no longer distant and peripheral concerns. In 747 the Tang had sent an army under the renowned Korean general Kao Xienqi to pacify the west; he had defeated the Tibetans and taken over governance of the region. In 750 he got involved in a regional dispute and marched into Ferghana in western Turkestan, decapitating a local ruler whose son fled to seek Arab support.

The Karluk defection

This was the excuse the Arabs had been waiting for, and an army under Ziyad ibn Salih, which included Tibetan and Uighur forces, marched on the Chinese frontier. Kao mobilized his force of 30-100,000 men (depending on whether the source is Chinese or Islamic), supported by Karluk (or Qarluq) Turks, and met them at Talas (probably not the modern town of that name but near Jambul, in modern-day Kazakhstan). After a five day battle the Karluks switched sides and Kao's army was routed. According to 13/14th-century Islamic historian al-Dhahabi, "God cast terror into the hearts of the Chinese. Victory descended, and the unbelievers were put to flight." Kao escaped back to China, and thousands of his troops tried to flee, with many captured and taken as prisoners to Samarkand.

The destruction of Chinese forces in the area enabled the Tibetans to seize control of the Tarim Basin, while the Tang Dynasty found itself occupied with a massive uprising back in China. Severely weakened thenceforth, the Tang were never able to reestablish control over their western territories, and instead the western Turks were absorbed into the Islamic world. According to Thaalibi, the 11th-century Arab author of *The Book of Curious and Entertaining Information*, Chinese prisoners revealed the secret of papermaking, transforming Samarkand into a center for paper production, from where the technology spread rapidly through the Islamic world to Europe. Archaeological finds clearly show that paper was being made in this region before Talas, but the Arab victory and subsequent hegemony accelerated the spread of paper westward.

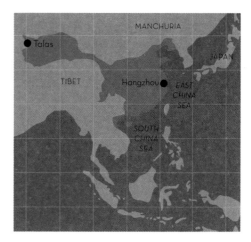

▲ The extent of the Tang empire ca. 700, showing how Chinese control had extended far into the West.

800

Year that Charlemagne was crowned emperor

Charlemagne ("Charles the Great") was a Frankish king of the Carolingian Dynasty who conquered most of Western Europe and eventually laid claim to the imperial throne of Rome. Charles was born in 742; his father was Pepin the Short, the real power behind the Merovingians, nominal kings of the Franks. In 751 Pepin finally deposed the last Merovingian king, Childeric III, and was crowned king by the Pope, forging a close relationship between the papacy and his new Carolingian Dynasty. On his death in 768 the Frankish kingdom was divided between his two sons, but when Carloman died in 771 the remaining son, Charles, became sole ruler of the Franks.

At over 6 feet (1.8 m) tall, Charles was strong and impressive, and although he never learned to read he could speak Latin and some Greek, and had a keen appreciation of the power of scholarship and culture, along with a driving ambition to achieve control over the lands of the former Roman empire. The Church would be a key tool in his agenda, and he worked to reform it into a powerful instrument of state control.

The Carolingian Renaissance

From 772 Charles launched his conquest of Europe, conquering the pagan tribes of Germany and converting them to Christianity at the point of a sword. First he conquered the Lombards and gained control of northern Italy and the Adriatic coast. In the late

770s an attempt to invade Spain was rebuffed, but his conquest of Saxony was relentless, reaching a gory climax at Verden in 782 when he was said to have executed 4,500 prisoners. At the same time Charles instituted a cultural renaissance based around his court at Aachen, to which he invited leading scholars such as Alcuin of York and Paul the Deacon.

Emperor of the Romans

His crowning glory came after internecine intrigue in the Byzantine empire led to the blinding and deposition of the emperor Constantine by his own mother, Irene, in 796. She declared herself emperor, but Alcuin of York insisted that in fact the imperial seat was now vacant, and so at Rome, on Christmas Day in the year 800, Charlemagne had his puppet Pope Leo III crown him Emperor of the Romans. The reach of Charlemagne's power and reputation at this time is illustrated by the arrival that year of an embassy from the Abbasid caliph Haroun al-Rashid, bearing gifts from far-off Baghdad.

In 813 the ailing Charlemagne had his son Louis the Pious crowned co-emperor, and the following year he died, leaving to Louis suzerainty over lands stretching from the Pyrenees to the shores of the Baltic Sea, and from the English Channel to the Adriatic coast of Dalmatia. The vast Carolingian empire did not long survive him, however; Louis' weakness and the squabbling of his sons meant that the empire was subdivided. The title of Emperor, however, would be passed on to a succession of German rulers until it lapsed during the Napoleonic Wars of the early 19th century.

▼ Albrecht Dürer's splendid imagining of Charlemagne in his imperial robes and regalia, some 700 years after the fact.

846

Rise of the Cholas

In the year 846 the Chola king Vijayalaya captured Tanjore from the Pandyas, marking the emergence of a new power in South India that would eventually conquer and unite a large part of the subcontinent. The Cholas were a Tamil people who had ruled a small kingdom in southern India since the 1st century CE, but were under the suzerainty of the Pallavas. At this time South India was a patchwork of competing states and empires, with the Pallavas of Kanchipuram, the Chalukyas of Badami, and the Pandyas of Madurai constantly striving to get the upper hand.

In the late 9th century the rise of the Cholas was greatly helped by fighting between the other powers, which cleared their way. The Chalukya king Vijayaditya III scored major successes against the Pallava and Pandya, enabling the Chola king, Aditya I (870–ca. 906), to conquer first the Pallavas and then the Pandyas. Eventually the Chalukyas themselves would be absorbed into the Chola empire, which reached its apogee under Rajaraja I (ruled 985–1014), and his successor Rajendra (ruled 1014–1044). In 994 Rajaraja conquered the Cheras and Pandyas, unifying the southern peninsula and invading Sri Lanka, and advancing as far north as the Ganges.

Chola rule of South India saw Tamil culture flourish and mature, while Chola sculpture, painting, and architecture are said to represent the apogee of classical South Indian culture. The empire quickly receded from its high point under Rajendra and was eventually destroyed in the 13th century.

▲ Rajendra Chola crowned with a garland by Shiva; in fact he was known as the Thrice-Crowned Chola for the kingdoms he had conquered.

869

Year of last inscription at Tikal

The last dated inscription on a stela (stone tablet) at the Maya city of Tikal is from the year 869 (around 10.1.19.15.10 in the Maya Long Count calendar). Tikal was the greatest city during the greatest phase of Maya civilization, the Classic period, and the date on this stelae gives an approximate bound on the date of its decline. Last recorded inscriptions from other Classic Maya cities paint a picture of a wave of devastation rolling across the Classic Maya heartland: Quiriguá, 810; Copán, 822; Caracol, 859; Tikal, 869; and finally Toniná in modern-day Mexico, 909.

The vanishing city

Tikal's collapse was so complete that it vanished almost entirely from human ken. When Hernán Cortés marched through the region in 1525, he passed within a few miles of the city without being aware of it. An extensive survey of dozens of Maya sites in 1841 by explorers John Lloyd Stephens and Frederick Catherwood failed to spot Tikal. Yet a relatively short time before this, Tikal was a huge, densely populated city of around 60,000 souls. The mystery of its decline, described by archaeologist Robert Sharer as "one of the most profound cultural failures in human history," may proffer a grim warning to modern civilization.

Tikal is an abandoned, ruined city in Guatemala. The name *Tikal*, meaning "at the waterhole," is a reference to natural reservoirs that the Maya enlarged: extraordinary feats of hydrological engineering that made their civilization possible. But it is a relatively modern name; inscriptions, known as glyphs, at the site show that the Maya called the city Yax Mutul.

Settlement at Tikal dates back to 800 BCE, but the heart of the city, the Great Plaza, was not laid down until around 200 BCE. The city flourished during the Classic period of Maya civilization (around 250-900 CE), with an initial period of success in the 4th-6th centuries, followed by a period from the late 6th century to 672 CE, known as the Tikal Hiatus, in which few inscriptions were made. During the 8th century the city was at its height. Over 3,000 buildings were erected on raised platforms or acropolises around the city center, including giant stepped-pyramids up to 212 feet (64 m) high, palaces (government buildings), observatories, ball courts, causeways, and homes. The city grew until it covered more than 20 square miles (52 sq km)—47 sq miles (122 sq km) according to some estimates—and its population swelled to 60,000 or more.

The end

The Guatemalan lowlands seem lush but in practice they make poor farmland, with erratic water supplies and large areas where soil fertility is only very slowly renewed once depleted. In order to feed the population, the Maya employed a range of clever techniques, from enlarging natural basins to harvest and husband the often scant rainfall, to intensive, water-efficient agricultural techniques. But as the city swelled the Tikal Maya started to exploit marginal land that was quickly exhausted, even as their unsustainable use of natural resources such as timber led to deforestation and soil erosion. The 9th century saw the onset of a dry period with a number of severe droughts, and this must have pushed the environmentally stressed region over the edge. Many great buildings at Tikal were burned as Classic Maya cities across the region collapsed. Survivors moved on to other parts of Central America, where Maya civilization endured until the arrival of the conquistadors in the 16th century, leaving Tikal as a magnificent ruin.

887

Moai on Easter Island

There are 887 colossal statues or *moai* on Easter Island, known to its indigenous inhabitants as Rapa Nui, an isolated island in the Pacific, over 2,500 miles (4,000 km) from Chile to the east and 2,000 miles (3,200 km) from Tahiti in the west. Some moai stand on platforms call *ahu*, but most still rest in the quarry where they were carved. Emblematic of the enduring mysteries of Easter Island, the moai may also have been the cause of the catastrophic collapse of the island's ecology and society.

The moai are carved from volcanic tuff (hardened volcanic ash), which is relatively easily worked. They probably represent chiefs and/or ancestors, and may have served to mediate between heaven and earth, although no one really knows because by the time the first European explorers arrived in 1722 the indigenous civilization had already collapsed, and the population rapidly dwindled thereafter. Most of the moai were probably carved between 1400 and 1600 CE. Of the 887, only 288 actually made it to an *ahu*; 397 still lie in the Rano Raraku quarry where they were carved, with a further 92 lying on roads from the quarry. On average the moai are 13 feet (4 m) high and weigh 14 tons (12.7 tonnes). When Captain Cook visited the island in 1774, most of the moai had been toppled, and it is believed that the need for timber to transport the colossi led to deforestation and ecological and societal collapse, causing a revolt against the ruling chiefs and priests in which the statues were pushed over.

▼ Easter Island moai; contrary to popular belief, these statues are not just heads—they also have bodies, which generally extend to the top of the legs.

1000

The Millennium

In 525 CE, the Scythian monk Dionysius Exiguus (aka Dennis the Short) introduced the *Anno Domini* system of counting years, stating that it was now the "525th year since the incarnation of Our Lord Jesus Christ." At the time the prevailing dating system described the current time as the year 247, and one suggestion is that Dionysius was motivated by a desire to stop people 250 years into the future from worrying that the End Times would soon be upon them, since there was a strain of Christian eschatology (the study of the End Times, including the Apocalypse and the Day of Judgment) which said that the Second Coming would be 500 years after the first one. By skipping the year 500 and going straight to 525, the theory goes, Dionysus was performing the eschatological equivalent of passing Go without collecting $200, circumventing the problem entirely.

The End of Days

Dionysius' AD system risked simply pushing the problem back by around five centuries, however, since 1000 is a date that lends itself neatly to eschatological associations. According to the Book of Revelations, the Second Coming would occur "after the Devil has been bound for 1,000 years," after which Christ would rule the Earth for another thousand years. This latter period is what is meant in Christian theology by the Millennium, and it is followed by the Apocalypse and the Last Judgment. Later Protestant sects

believed in the literal reality of the Millennium, and early Christians probably did too. But did people around the year 1000 CE believe by association that the end of a calendar millennium had vast eschatological significance?

▲ Detail of Michelangelo's *Last Judgment*, in the Vatican's Sistine Chapel.

Evidence gap

Suggestions that they did date almost exclusively to long after the period. The first known mention of millennial panic comes from the German abbot Johannes Trithemius in around 1500: "many... feared that the last day was at hand... deluded by a false calculation that the visible world would end in the year 1000."

Belief in millennial panic became received wisdom, usually in the context of a progressive view of history in which the enlightened present looks back on the irrational and benighted past. But even in the 19th century, some historians questioned the reality of the millennial panic, given the total lack of contemporary historical evidence, and the mainstream view today is that it never happened. According to Bernard McGinn, author of the 1969 *Encyclopedia of Apocalypticism*, "'Medieval folk lived in a more or less constant state of apocalyptic expectation [so] it is by no means clear that fears of the end were more general circa 1000 than at other periods in the Middle Ages."

1788

First Fleet arrives in Australia

Australia's traditional founding date is January 26th, 1788. This was the day that the First Fleet sailed into Port Jackson harbor and landed at Sydney Cove to start a settlement of convicts and their guardians. Today January 26th is celebrated as Australia Day, although for many Aborigines it is mourned as a dark day.

Plans to set up a penal colony in Australia developed after the loss of the American colonies following the American Revolution, which meant that Britain could no longer ship convicts there from her overcrowded prisons. Sir Joseph Banks, who had visited New South Wales in Australia with Captain Cook, suggested that Botany Bay would make the perfect site, and in 1784 the British government passed "An Act for the Effectual Transportation of Felons and Other Offenders," which allowed it to choose "some place beyond the seas" as a penal colony. On May 13th, 1787, the First Fleet set sail under Captain Arthur Phillip. On board the transports were 500 male and 250 female convicts; 23 of them would die on the voyage, along with one marine.

After 36 weeks the Fleet arrived at Botany Bay, only to discover that it was not at all suitable. Instead they moved north to Port Jackson, where Phillip picked out a suitable cove, which he named for his friend Lord Sydney. Including marines and their families, 1023 colonists went ashore. Over the next 80 years, 158,829 convicts would be transported, with the last ship arriving in Western Australia on January 9th, 1868.

1939

Start of World War II

World War II was the largest conflict in human history, but at its outset in 1939 it could still be seen as a European struggle in the mode of Great Power conflicts of an earlier era. The roots of the war lay in the Great Depression of the 1930s. On the one hand the Depression sapped the ability and appetite of powers such as the US, Britain, and France for rearmament and military action; on the other it exacerbated the grievances and woes of those countries that had suffered in the Peace of Paris that concluded World War I.

▼ A woman from Sudetenland tearfully gives the Nazi salute, in an image that was used by the USA to warn of the perils of "Hitlerism."

Last chance at Stresa

In Germany the Depression led to economic breakdown and social upheaval, paving the way for Hitler and the Nazis to seize dictatorial power from 1933. Hitler had already laid out his vision of the future for Germany, which involved redressing the injustices of the Treaty of Versailles and seizing *Lebensraum* ("living space"), through the occupation and "ruthless Germanization" of territory in the east. Almost immediately Germany began rearming in contravention of Treaty restrictions, and in March 1935, Hitler announced the resumption of conscription and the reestablishment of the Luftwaffe.

In April, at a meeting at Stresa, in Italy, Britain, France, and Italy united to condemn these moves and affirm the independence of Austria, an obvious target for the Austrian-born Hitler. But in what

now looks like a turning point in history, the "Stresa Front" quickly broke up. Britain and France objected to the Italian invasion of Ethiopia, driving Mussolini decisively into bed with Hitler, and Britain limply conceded that Germany should be allowed to rearm its navy. German military reoccupation of the Rhineland went unopposed. If Hitler needed any more assurance that aggression would be met with appeasement, it was apparent in the weakness of British and French support for the Republicans in the Spanish Civil War, in the face of blatant German and Italian arming of the Fascists.

The failure of appeasement

Accordingly Britain and France acceded to Hitler's forced union of Germany and Austria in March 1938, and condoned his seizure of the Sudetenland from Czechoslovakia in late 1938. Once more opting for appeasement, Britain and France trusted Hitler's assurances that he would respect the sovereignty of the rest of Czechoslovakia. In March 1939 these assurances turned to dust, as the Germans marched unopposed into the Czech provinces of Bohemia and Moravia, and shortly afterward annexed part of Lithuania.

It was finally evident that appeasement would not work, and Britain and France agreed to guarantee the independence of Poland, which was clearly next in the firing line. Only now did the allies begin to rearm, but Hitler's grand plan was already in motion. Calculating that the French would not venture beyond their vaunted Maginot Line and that Belgian neutrality would prevent attack from that quarter, he massed his forces to the east. The final piece of his plan fell into place on 23rd August, 1939, when the Soviet Union agreed to a Non-Aggression Pact, with a secret coda agreeing the partition of Poland. Six days later the Germans invaded Poland, and two days after that France and Britain declared war on Germany.

▲ Hitler and other leading Nazis in Vienna, shortly after the Anschluss, the union of Austria and Germany.

1947

Partition and independence of India and Pakistan

During World War II, Britain tried to put India's drive for independence firmly on hold, and when this failed Churchill sent Sir Stafford Cripps on a mission to India in 1942. Cripps offered Gandhi and Jawaharlal Nehru a deal: in return for Indian support in prosecuting the war, India would be given full Dominion status (autonomy) after the war. Gandhi rejected the offer as "a post-dated check on a bank that was failing" and instead the British imposed martial law and ruthlessly crushed dissent. But the genie was now out of the bottle, and it was clear that when the war was over Britain would have to withdraw from India. In October 1946 the Viceroy, Lord Wavell, would note in his diary: "Our time in India is limited, and our power to control events almost gone." When the new Labour government came into office in Britain after the war, it was more determined than ever to get out of India.

The handover of power, however, faced an intractable problem: Hindu–Muslim tensions. Nehru and his Congress Party were determined that India should not be split up, and that the government they were likely to lead would rule the whole country. The Muslim League, under Muhammad Ali Jinnah, viewed being a permanent minority, subject to a perpetual Hindu majority, as intolerable. Jinnah

▼ Gandhi with Lord and Lady Mountbatten. Louis Mountbatten would be the last Viceroy and First Governor-General of India.

wanted an independent Muslim nation, or at the very least a high degree of autonomy for Muslim provinces in a loose federation. But Congress saw a strong central authority as the only viable means of governing the country.

Communal massacres

In 1946 these divisions took on a terrible dimension. Exacerbated by riots over food shortages, Hindu-Muslim violence flared and communal massacres broke out all over the country. India was slipping into bloody civil breakdown and sectarian war. The British tried to force the pace of the independence negotiations. The British Prime Minister, Clement Attlee, set June 1948 as a deadline, while the new Viceroy, Lord Mountbatten, felt compelled to bring this forward to August 1947, and decided that partition was inevitable. India would be broken up into a central Hindu state flanked by two wings of a Muslim state, East and West Pakistan, comprising parts of Bengal and Punjab provinces, respectively. East Pakistan would later become Bangladesh.

In July 1947, the British Parliament passed the Indian Independence Act, which ordered that the dominions of India and Pakistan be demarcated by midnight of August 14-15th, 1947. Boundary commissioners raced to partition Punjab and Bengal, trying to draw borders that would separate the majority of Hindus from the majority of Muslims, but the drawing of boundaries simply precipitated one of the largest mass movements in history. Fearing ending up on the "wrong side" of the new border, 15 million Hindus, Muslims, and Sikhs fled their homes, and up to a million died in horrific communal massacres. Under Nehru's stewardship, however, India would go on to become the world's largest democracy.

A victim of fanaticism

Gandhi was appalled by the violence that followed partition and tried to calm the massacres by walking through some of the worst-hit regions. Despite his efforts, he could not stop an undeclared war breaking out between the two new countries in Kashmir, and on January 30th, 1948, he was gunned down by a Hindu fanatic.

1956

Suez Crisis

The Suez Crisis was an international incident centered on the Suez Canal, in which Britain and France colluded with Israel in an attempt to humiliate Egypt's President Gamal Abdel Nasser, only for the roles to be reversed. Nasser had come to power in Egypt from 1952, making himself president in 1956. His position was delicate. Partly to help prosecute his anti-Israeli policy—which had seen him establish guerrilla bases in the Sinai Peninsula to mount raids into Israel, and close to Israeli shipping in the Straits of Tiran, at the southern end of the Red Sea—he wanted to buy arms, and the only place he could get them was from the Eastern Bloc. In September 1955 he had agreed a huge arms deal with Czechoslovakia. But at the same time he needed money from the West to fund the Aswan Dam project. His deal for Communist weapons helped convince the Americans to back out of funding the dam, and in July 1956 they pulled their support.

▲ The location of the Suez Canal, which runs between Port Said in the north and Suez in the South.

Nationalizing the Canal

A week later, Nasser announced that he was nationalizing the Suez Canal Company, which operated the Canal, and in which the British and French had extensive interests. Nasser was careful not to breach the terms of the international treaty governing the running of the Canal, but opposition to him personally was strong in France, and particularly in Britain. Accordingly the British and French began planning military action designed to humiliate

Nasser, despite American opposition. Israel, too, was keen to act against Egypt. A plan was agreed whereby Israel would commit ground troops and French and British ships and planes would negate the Egyptians' naval or air forces.

On October 29th, 1956, Israeli forces swept into the Sinai and advanced on the Canal. The threat from British and French forces kept the Egyptian planes on the ground. Britain and France then used a UN call for a ceasefire to demand that both Egypt and Israel withdraw from the sides of the Canal, and on November 5th and 6th they began occupying the canal zone.

▲ Smoke rises from oil tanks beside the Suez Canal, during the initial Anglo-French assault on Port Said, November 5th, 1956.

But they had horribly miscalculated the American reaction. Partly to head off Soviet threats of intervention, the USA sponsored UN resolutions against the Anglo-French venture, and the Americans refused to intervene to halt a run on the British pound sterling, caused solely by British involvement in the crisis. Britain immediately called off the military action, and she and France were forced to pull out of Egypt, humiliated, and in the case of Britain some $400 million poorer, prompting the diplomat and writer Sir Harold Nicolson to describe the Suez affair as "a smash and grab raid that was all smash and no grab." Nasser became a national and pan-Arabic hero. Israel had to withdraw, but in fact had secured the objectives of clearing the guerrilla bases and reopening the Straits of Tiran. France was left with an abiding distrust of the Anglo-American axis and turned her face toward Europe, hastening the formation of the European Community. Britain's lingering imperial pretensions were in tatters (Prime Minister Eden was forced to resign), and British and French influence in the Middle East evaporated.

1966

The Great Proletarian Cultural Revolution

The Great Proletarian Cultural Revolution, (in Chinese: *Wu-ch'an Chieh-chi Wen-hua Ta Ke-ming*), better known as simply the Cultural Revolution, was a mass movement in China instituted by Mao Zedong to purge what he called "capitalist roaders" and achieve his vision of a purified Maoist Communism.

Mao's Great Leap Forward, an attempt to revolutionize Chinese economic development between 1956 and 1960, had been a disastrous failure and he was forced to step aside as Chairman of the Republic. At the same time relations with the Soviets had soured. Mao feared the Chinese revolution would ossify, like the Soviet one, into a centralized, industrialized technocracy. Clinging to agrarian utopian visions and fearing for his legacy, while at the same time resentful of being sidelined and treated, as he put it, "like a dead ancestor," Mao decided to shake up the Chinese Communist Party and give the youth of the nation their own taste of revolution.

▼ A group of Chinese children in uniform in front of a picture of Chairman Mao, each holding a copy of his "Little Red Book," during the Cultural Revolution.

The Great Helmsman

In 1966 he ordered the urban youth of China to organize into Red Guard militias and purge all the "capitalist roaders" (those who followed the path of capitalism). They were publicly to criticize intellectuals, suspect party members, and anyone guilty of supposed capitalist transgressions. The cult of Mao himself, the "Great Helmsman," was elevated to manic fervor. In 1967, in the

"January Revolution," the Red Guard attempted to seize control of all Party organizations, but they quickly spiraled out of control, terrorizing and killing thousands, and descending into anarchic warfare and sectionalism. Red Guard thugs battled People's Liberation Army (PLA) soldiers in the streets, destroyed cultural monuments and institutions ancient and modern, and stormed foreign embassies, and by September Mao was forced to order the PLA to suppress them, although this was not accomplished until the summer of 1968.

The Gang of Four

The Cultural Revolution continued until 1976, but behind the scenes a fierce power struggle played out for control of the Party and the country. This reached a head a month after Mao's death in September 1976, when the radicals pushing the Cultural Revolution agenda, known as the Gang of Four, were arrested by Mao's successor Hua Guofeng. This marked the end of the Revolution. Opinions diverge radically on the extent of the economic damage done by the Cultural Revolution. According to some sources it took 20 years for the Chinese economy to recover, but a dissenting view is that the damage was transient. Grain production fell in 1968, but it had risen in the preceding two years and did so again afterward. Industrial production plunged by 13 percent between 1966 and 1968, but had fully recovered by 1971.

The most severe setbacks

The cultural, institutional, and human damage wrought by the Cultural Revolution was incontrovertible. Universities, for instance, were closed between 1966 and 1970; about 70 percent of Party officials were purged, with 3 million sent to labor in the countryside, alongside 17 million students, 10 million of whom were still there in 1978. Around 500,000 people were killed and over 100 million were terrorized in one way or another. An official statement in 1981 accused the Cultural Revolution of having caused "the most severe setbacks and the heaviest losses suffered by the Party, the state, and the people since the foundation of the People's Republic."

1989

Freedom and repression

In 1989 a wave of democratization, sometimes known as the Autumn of Nations or the Revolutions of '89, swept across Central and Eastern Europe, causing the collapse of the Eastern Bloc. Nowhere was this metaphorical tearing down of the Iron Curtain made more literal than in Berlin, where the fall of the Berlin Wall provided one of the most iconic moments in 20th-century history.

▼ People crowd onto the top of the Berlin Wall, near the Brandenburg Gate, on November 9th, 1989.

The fall of the Berlin Wall

The Berlin Wall had been erected in 1961, by an East German state (the German Democratic Republic [GDR]) desperate to prevent the hemorrhage of its citizens. Between 1955 and 1961 over 200,000 East Germans had fled to the West, and one of the easiest ways to do it was to cross into West Berlin. Thanks to the wartime settlement of the 1944 London Protocol, West Berlin had remained separate from the rest of East Germany, an enclave of freedom in a sea of Communist repression. The Soviets and their East German clients were determined to close its borders, and, starting on the night of August 12th–13th, police and worker militias set up 97 miles (155 km) of barbed wire fences around West Berlin, to be replaced over the following months with brick and concrete walls. Only seven of the 81 border crossings between East and West Berlin remained open. The GDR called it the *antifaschistischer Schutzwall* ("anti-Fascist protection wall"), but its self-evident role was to keep their citizens in.

Superpower face-offs over West Berlin were not infrequent, and some Western leaders may not have been too dismayed about the Wall. John F. Kennedy allegedly remarked that "a wall is a hell of a lot better than a war." Over the next 38 years about 5,000 East Germans made it through, over, under, or around the Wall, but another 5,000 were caught trying and 191 were shot dead. In 1989, as demonstrations and regime collapse swept across the Eastern Bloc, the GDR government scrambled to appease protestors and on November 9th, 1989, a Politburo member announced a relaxation of travel laws. Thousands of East Germans rushed to the Wall and bemused guards opened the crossings; people with sledgehammers started to demolish it and over the following months bulldozers completed the task.

Tiananmen Square

The Revolutions of '89 helped inspire a mass movement already underway in China. Student-led protests in 1986 and '87 resulted in a crackdown, in which the reforming Chinese Communist Party general secretary Hu Yaobang was forced to resign. His death in April 1989 sparked massive demonstrations, with students and other protestors gathering in Tiananmen Square in central Beijing. In mid-May a million people protested there, in front of the world's media. Deng Xiaoping and other elderly Party leaders feared that the student revolt would turn into another Cultural Revolution, and they ordered that the uprising be put down with military force. On the night of June 3th–4th, the protests were crushed. Officially 241 people, including soldiers, were killed, but the real death toll was probably 600–1,200, with up to 10,000 injured. The demonstrators in the Square itself were allowed to disperse peacefully, but many of those involved were later arrested and some were executed. Even today, the Chinese government ruthlessly suppresses all mention of the Tiananmen Square incident.

▼ A group of Chinese Army tanks blocks an overpass on Chang'an Avenue leading to Tiananmen Square, June 4th, 1989.

2003

The Iraq War

During the 2003 Iraq War, also known as the Second Persian Gulf War, the normal progress of warfare was inverted. The initial combat phase was quick and relatively bloodless, at least for the Americans and their allies, but victory proved far less so.

In the First Persian Gulf War, a UN-sanctioned coalition led by America defeated Saddam Hussein's Iraqi forces relatively easily, but stopped short of effecting regime change. Saddam clung on to power through brutal suppression of opponents, and pursued research into weapons of mass destruction. His refusal to allow proper monitoring by UN weapons inspectors led to U.S. bombing, and after the 9/11 attacks American appetite for direct military action increased, especially when the Bush administration erroneously linked Saddam's regime to Al Qaeda. The UN passed a new resolution threatening force, and the Iraqis appeared to cooperate, but George W. Bush and his British ally Tony Blair determined to topple Saddam, regardless of UN authorization.

On March 20th, 2003, the coalition attack began, and by April 9th U.S. soldiers had taken Baghdad and the Iraqi regime had collapsed. Saddam himself was captured on December 13th, and later executed. On May 1st, Bush declared major combat operations complete; at this time coalition casualties included just 150 deaths. Over the next six years over 4,000 more coalition troops would die. Estimates of the number of Iraqis killed vary widely, from 650,000 to 85,000 (although this latter figure, from the Iraqi government, refers only to the period 2004-08).

2010

The Arab Spring

Beginning at the end of 2010, a wave of pro-democracy protests and uprisings spread across North Africa and the Middle East, coming to be known as the Arab Spring. The trigger for the Arab Spring came in Tunisia on December 17th, 2010, when a street vendor named Mohamed Bouazizi set fire to himself to protest his mistreatment by the authorities. He died of his injuries on January 4th, 2011. Bouazizi's dramatic act sparked demonstrations and a protest movement dubbed the "Jasmine Revolution." Despite initial violent repression from the security forces, by the end of the month the Tunisian dictator Zine al-Abidine Ben Ali was forced to flee the country, which later made the transition to democracy.

The movement in Tunisia touched off massive protests in Egypt, centered on Tahrir Square in Cairo, which eventually led to the downfall of President Hosni Mubarak after nearly 30 years in power. From late January to March 2011, Arab Spring protests spread to Yemen, Bahrain, Libya, and Syria. In Libya the protests turned into an armed revolt, which saw Mu'ammar Gaddhafi toppled after NATO intervention on the side of the rebels. Gaddhafi was forced out of Tripoli in August and was captured and killed in Surt in October. In Syria, protests also turned into armed insurrection, and the entire country descended into a protracted and bloody civil war.

Demonstrations in Algeria, Morocco, Oman, and Jordan did not progress to full-blown uprisings, perhaps because the rulers of these countries offered concessions; it is also notable that

monarchs tended to survive better than republican dictators. Arab Spring movements in Yemen and Bahrain broke down or were brutally suppressed. In fact the failure of the Arab Spring movement to lead to lasting changes anywhere other than in Tunisia led to the reactionary response being labeled the Arab Autumn or Arab Winter. The primary outcome of the Arab Spring across most of the region has been an increase in instability and conflict, the rise of religious extremism and sectarian conflict, mass displacement of peoples, and hundreds of thousands of casualties.

▲ Protestors gather in Tahrir Square in Cairo, in December 2011.

5,126

Length of the Mayan
Long Count (years)

The Mayan Long Count is part of the complex and sophisticated Maya calendrical system. Most dates in Maya inscriptions are identified by where they fall within two concurrent cycles, the 260-day *tzolk'in* or sacred year and the 360-day solar year, or *haab'*. Combining these cycles shows that every 52 *haab'* years, the cycle repeats so that a given day will have the same *tzolk'in* and *haab'* names as 52 years earlier. Dating events that occurred more than 52 years ago therefore requires a different system, and for this the Maya developed a Long Count system analogous to the modern-day Julian year, where the date might be given as 21.12.12, indicating the 12th day of the 12th month in the year 2012. Maya mathematics is not decimal but vigesimal (base 20), so 20 days or *k'ins* give a *uinal*. A year or *tun* is 18 *uinals* or 360 days; 20 *tuns* give a *k'atun* (7,200 days); and 20 *k'atuns* give a *b'ak'tun* (144,000 days). This calendar ran from a specific starting date, 13.0.0.0.0, which equates in the Common Era system to 3114 BCE.

Because the Long Count is cyclical, it resets to the equivalent of zero after 13 *b'ak'tun* (about 5,125 solar years), which mean that the "end" of the Long Count fell in December 2012. Great upheavals and changes were promised but none materialized. In fact, on this date the Long Count system was simply due to reset to 13.0.0.0.0. The Maya had coefficients larger than a *b'ak'tun*, with the biggest, the *alautun*, equal to 23,040,000,000 days. The alautun era will not finish until roughly 63,078,286 CE.

⬭	•	••	•••	••••
0	1	2	3	4

—	•	••	•••	••••
5	6	7	8	9

═	•	••	•••	••••
10	11	12	13	14

☰	•	••	•••	••••
15	16	17	18	19

▲ Along with their sophisticated calendar, the Maya are celebrated for mathematical achievements such as independently inventing the zero, seen here with other Maya numerals.

10,000

Price of a Semper
Augustus (guilders)

Tulips, grown from bulbs, were valued commodities in the Netherlands in the 1630s, and the selling by weight of bulbs that were still in the ground, and would therefore be expected to grow, encouraged speculation. By 1636 a futures market for tulip bulbs had developed, and trading became increasingly frenzied. The ensuing financial bubble became known as "tulipmania."

At the height of the frenzy, bulbs weighing 1 oz (14 g) were selling for 3,000 guilders. According to a contemporary pamphlet, the value of such a sum was equivalent to, among other things: eight pigs, four oxen, 12 sheep, 24 tons of wheat, 100 pounds of cheese, a silver drinking cup, and possibly even a ship. Bulbs of the most valuable tulip, a striking red and white variegated flower called the Semper Augustus, were being touted for sale in February 1637 for 10,000 guilders, a sum that would have fed and clothed a family for life.

In fact such a price was never met, and the highest amount recorded as being offered for a single bulb was for a variety called Violetten Admirael van Enkhuizen, which sold on February 5th, 1637, for 5,200 guilders. For comparison, in 1642 Rembrandt charged 1,600 guilders for his massive painting *The Night Watch*.

The market, however, was already collapsing; an auction two days before this in Haarlem had seen no bidders, and the trades made at Alkmaar were never honored. This ensured that only a few among the small and well-off portion of the Dutch population that had engaged in tulipmania were ruined in the crash.

▼ Illustration of the Semper Augustus tulip, the most valuable variety at the height of tulipmania.

13,418

Places catalogued in the Domesday Book

The Domesday Book is the earliest surviving public record in Britain and probably the most remarkable bureaucratic achievement of early medieval Europe. In fact it is two books, known as Great and Little Domesday. The name "Domesday" refers to the Day of Judgment, for it was said that just as nothing could be hidden from God's final judgment, so nothing could be hidden from the surveyors of King William, who had commissioned the Book to determine who owned what in his new kingdom. The first recorded use of the name Domesday Book comes from around 1170; at the time it was written it may have been known as "The Great Survey," "The Book of Winchester" (where the survey was originally kept), or "The Great Description of England."

It seemed no shame

Domesday was commissioned by William the Conqueror at Gloucester at Christmas 1085. Fearful of a Danish invasion, he was raising an army and wanted to work out how much he and his nobles could afford to pay. The following year, teams of commissioners went across the land, questioning landowners and villagers and recording land areas, tax rates, livestock holdings, and many other details. An Anglo-Saxon chronicler recorded that: "[William] sent his men all over England into every shire... Also he had a record made of... how much everybody had who was occupying land in England, in land or cattle, and how much money it was worth. So very narrowly did he have it investigated, that there was no single hide nor a yard of land, nor indeed (it is a shame to relate but it seemed no shame to him to do) one ox nor one cow nor one pig which was there left out, and not put down in his record: and all these records were brought to him afterward."

A lot of sheep

The collated data was edited into a huge book, the Great Domesday, although the raw data for Essex, Norfolk, and Suffolk was, for some reason, not condensed, and remained as a separate book, the Little Domesday. Great Domesday comprises 2 million words written on 913 pages of vellum (from around a thousand sheep), mentioning 13,418 places, and written out by a single clerk (Little Domesday was written by up to seven clerks). The combined volumes miss out some significant portions of the country, including much of northern England and the two most important cities in the realm, London and Winchester. It records the (male) heads of households, but misses out their wives and children.

A significant feature of Domesday is how it reflected and facilitated the way that William and the Norman conquest were recasting England as a feudal society. Although the material had been collected in geographic order, with commissioners visiting the county-town of each county in turn, and investigating each hundred (county division) and village, the data were then reorganized under the headings of the king and his tenants in chief, so that the basic unit became the honor or barony—the set of estates held by a noble, even when they were not adjacent.

▲ Fanciful depiction of William the Conqueror, who would not have worn full plate armor.

15,000

Bulgarians blinded by Basil II

In 1014, in an act that shocked even his medieval contemporaries, the Byzantine emperor Basil II earned himself the byname *Bulgaroktonos*, "the Bulgar Slayer." One of the greatest and most indomitable of Byzantine emperors, Basil's early life reads like a novel. After the death in 963 of his father, Romanus II, he and his brother Constantine were officially co-emperors, but the senior imperial role was taken by the general Nicephorus Phocas, who married their mother Theophano. Nicephorus won great military victories, but was assassinated in 969 by his nephew, John Tzimisces, lover of Theophano. Tzimisces in turn scored brilliant victories but died suddenly in 976, after which Basil's great-uncle, the eunuch Basil the Chamberlain, seized the reins of power. Finally, in 985, Basil II achieved sole authority, with the help of Russian soldiers who went on to form his elite Varangian Guard. In 996 he launched the first in a series of campaigns against his greatest enemy, Samuel, tsar of the Bulgars. After nearly 20 years of warfare, Basil finally closed in on the Bulgar capital Ochrida. At Belasita in 1014 he won a great victory over the tsar's army, putting out the eyes of 15,000 captive Bulgars, leaving a single eye to each 100th man so that they might lead the rest back to Samuel, who was said to have died of shock. Basil Bulgarohktonos, as he became known, annexed Bulgaria by 1018, extended Byzantine control to the shores of Lake Van in Armenia, consolidated his power in southern Italy, and was planning the invasion of Sicily when he died in 1025.

19074

Serial number of the pistol used to assassinate Archduke Ferdinand

On June 28th, 1914, a shot rang out from a pistol with the serial number 19074, issued to the assassin Gavrilo Princip by a Serbian secret society, the Black Hand. The target was Archduke Franz Ferdinand, heir-apparent to the Austro-Hungarian imperial throne; his murder triggered World War I.

The Black Hand was the informal name for the terrorist organization "Unification or Death!" In 1908 the province of Bosnia had been annexed by the Austro-Hungarian empire, and the Black Hand believed that violent acts, especially targeted assassinations, would help accomplish the creation of Greater Serbia, including the unification of Serbia with Bosnia.

On June 28th, 1914, Franz Ferdinand paid an official visit to Sarajevo, capital of Bosnia. Equipped with grenades and pistols, Princip and five others determined to kill him. One of the group threw a grenade at Ferdinand's car, but the Archduke was not hurt. However, as he was being driven to the hospital to visit the wounded, Princip fired at Ferdinand from short range; the Archduke died shortly thereafter, along with his wife, Sophie.

Princip was arrested, tried, and sentenced to hard labor, but when the Black Hand ringleaders were identified and the Austrians demanded they be handed over, the Serb authorities refused. Austria-Hungary declared war on Serbia on July 28th, 1914, setting off a chain reaction of declarations by allies of each side until all of Europe was mired in a vast conflagration.

▲ The FN Model 1910 semi-automatic pistol used by Princip to assassinate Franz Ferdinand.

20,000

Desaparecidos

Between 1976 and 1983 Argentina was convulsed by a *Guerra Sucia*, or Dirty War, in which 10-30,000 people were made to "disappear." Abduction and torture were commonplace, and it later transpired that hundreds had been thrown from airplanes in mid-flight, to be eaten by sharks, while babies had been abducted and given to childless military couples.

The Dirty War arguably started two years earlier, when Argentine president Juan Perón died and was succeeded by his vice-president and widow, Isabelita Perón. Her chief advisor was extreme rightwinger, José López Rega, whose death squads killed over 2,000 people in late 1974. When Perón was deposed by a military coup in March 1976, a junta took control of Argentina and launched a concerted campaign to liquidate leftist elements.

Camps and torture prisons were established, and perceived dissidents, including pregnant women and children, were persecuted. Up to 30,000 of them were never seen again, presumably murdered; they came to be known as *los desaparacidos*, "the disappeared." From 1977 until 2006, mothers of the disappeared assembled in Buenos Aires' Plaza de Mayo every Thursday afternoon, displaying photographs of their missing children.

In 1983, the military junta was forced to cede power to a democratically elected government. Despite a few successful prosecutions, threats from the military weakened the government's resolve and led to most of those responsible escaping justice.

22,000

Price of the Danegeld
(pounds of silver)

In 991, the *Anglo-Saxon Chronicle* records the brave Byrhtnoth, an Ealdorman of King Aethelred the Unready (i.e. a high-ranking noble), was killed by the Vikings in a battle at Maldon, in Essex. Viking raids on England from both east and west threatened to destroy the Anglo-Saxon kingdom, and that same year Archbishop Sigeric had advised the King to make, or rather, purchase, peace. To pay off the Danes, Aethelred levied a *geld*, or royal tax, in the amount of 2 shillings per hide (a unit of land area equivalent to approximately 120 acres or ~50 hectares. The price of peace, agreed in a treaty with the Viking lord Olaf Tryggvason, was 22,000 pounds of silver. This payment was known at the time as a *gafol*. Byrhtnoth, though loyal to the king, vehemently opposed the *gafol*, and paid for this with his life.

Unfortunately the *gafol* was not a one-off. Every year the English were forced to raise another *geld*, and the amount kept rising. By 1007 the price was £30,000. Late payment could be even more costly; in 1011 Vikings captured Canterbury, murdered the Archbishop, and carried off £48,000—it was said the disaster was caused by late payment of the *gafol*.

Although the Danes themselves took control of England under Canute in 1016, and were later driven out altogether, kings found it useful to continue levying the annual tax. The tax was first called the Danegeld under the Normans, and it was last levied in 1162.

▲ Manuscript illustration showing Aethelred II, the Unready. His cognomen is a mistranslation of *unraed*, meaning "ill-advised."

25,000

Distance of the Long March (li)

The Long March was one of the greatest fighting retreats in history, in which Chinese Communist forces broke out of an encirclement and, over the course of a year between October 1934 and October 1935, fought their way across 25,000 *li* (about 6,000 miles [10,000 km]) of harsh terrain to Shaanxi in the northwest of China.

Bandit country

In 1934 Chinese Communist forces under Mao Zedong were surrounded by troops of the Kuomintang or Nationalist Party. Mao was replaced and his guerrilla tactics dropped, with disastrous consequences, as the Nationalists prosecuted a "bandit suppression campaign," encircling the Communists with over 700,000 troops. As their numbers dwindled the Communists planned a desperate breakout, and in October about 86,000 men and 30 women broke through the Nationalist lines. Harassed by air and ground forces, around half of the men were lost in the first three months, and in January 1935, at a conference at Zunyi, in the southwestern province of Guizhou, Mao was able to reestablish control of the party.

Although their numbers were swelled when a force of Communists arrived under Zhang Guotao, he and Mao clashed and Zhang led a substantial faction toward the far southwest. Meanwhile Mao headed for northern Shaanxi, where other

▲ Some of the survivors of the Long March made by Communist leader Mao Zedong and his followers from south to north China.

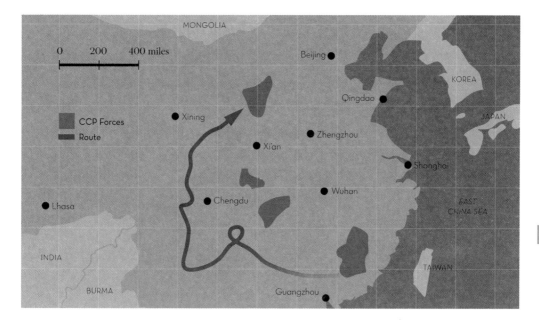

Communists had secured territory, and where the proximity of the Soviet border and Japanese forces offered a modicum of protection from the Nationalists.

By the time Mao and his forces arrived in Shaanxi, having crossed 18 mountain ranges and 24 rivers, there were just 8,000 survivors. These veterans of what came to be called the Long March joined up with local Communists and were later rejoined by some of the group who had earlier split off. In December 1936 Mao was able to mobilize around 30,000 troops to move to the Yan'an district, and here they remained throughout the Sino-Japanese War (1937–40).

The rigors of the Long March served to establish Mao as the preeminent Communist leader, providing the movement with a heroic legend and, in the Long March veterans, a contingent of secular saints. Many of latter did not survive Mao's Cultural Revolution, their sacrifice apparently insufficient to spare them brutal purging. The legend of the Long March lives on, however, for instance lending its name to China's space program, which in 2003 sent Yang Liwei, China's first astronaut, into orbit.

▲ The circuitous route of the Long March, which covered 6,000 miles (10,000 km).

57,471

Length of the Roman road
network (Roman miles)

The road network was one of ancient Rome's greatest achievements. At its peak under the emperor Diocletian (ruled 284–305), the network reached 57,471 Roman miles in length. A Roman mile was equivalent to 4852 feet (1479 m), thus the Roman road network covered over 52,816 miles (85,000 km).

Roman roads were designed primarily for military and state purposes, such as the rapid passage of soldiers, postal couriers, and government agents. Post could travel up to 50 miles (80 km) in 24 hours. Commercial and private traffic was restricted or barred from many roads. The roads were built to last, with sophisticated engineering, including flagstones underlaid with gravel and sand, to cope with ground movement and frost, and a top layer of concrete to give a smooth surface. One reason the roads were so straight was because of a 5th-century BCE law specifying that a curved section of road had to be 16 feet (4.9 m) wide, double the width of straight sections. Straight roads were thus much cheaper to build and maintain.

Roman roads were so advanced that they were not surpassed in Europe until the beginning of the 19th century. Even though the formal program of maintenance collapsed with the Western Roman Empire, some of the roads were used for well over 1,000 years. For instance, during construction of the great cathedral at Troyes in France (13th–16th centuries), stone from the Tonnerre quarries was hauled along the original Roman roads.

stones set in concrete

gravel and sand

small stones

large stones

drainage ditch

▲ Cross-section through a Roman road. The flagstones associated in the modern day with such roads would have been covered with a layer of concrete, since eroded.

100,000

Skulls stacked in a pyramid

Timur Leng, aka Timur the Lame or Tamerlane, was a Turkic conqueror from Transoxiana (roughly corresponding to modern-day Uzbekistan) who cut a swathe of destruction through Central, East, and South Asia between around 1360 and 1405. Although a patron of the arts and, he claimed, a man of great piety, he is chiefly remembered for his ruthless and bloodthirsty savagery. Wherever he went, reported the Arab historian Zaid Vosifi, "blood poured from people as from vessels."

How much of his cruelty was legendary and how much factual is unclear, but the tales about him are fantastically gory. Any who resisted his conquering army would be beheaded, and their skulls were used to build pyramids, towers, and even roads. Timur was said personally to supervise the slaughter, and also the process of ripping open the stomachs of merchants to search for any gold they might have swallowed. He was even said to mix by his own hand poisons for his adversaries.

His barbaric atrocities included the building of a wall with the corpses of 2,000 prisoners at Sistan in 1384; burying alive 4,000 Armenians in 1401; massacring 70,000 inhabitants of Isfahan in 1387; and murdering in cold blood 100,000 Indian captives at Delhi, stacking their skulls into a pyramid, in 1398. The slaughter at Delhi was so excessive that, according to the 16th-century Indo-Persian historian Abd-ul-Qadir Bada'uni, "those of the inhabitants who were left died (of famines and pestilence), while for two months not a bird moved wing in Delhi."

▼ Timur feasting near Samarkand, in the heart of his short-lived Timurid empire.

156,115

Allied troops landed
in Normandy

The D-Day Landings of June 6th, 1944, comprised the greatest amphibious assault in history and marked a major turning point in World War II. In the course of a single, epic day, 6,939 ships and landing craft, 11,590 aircraft, 195,701 naval personnel, and 156,115 troops (delivered by air and sea) took part.

The term "D-day" itself is generic to any military operation, signifying the day that an operation is launched, but then as now the day on which the Allied invasion of Normandy was launched was widely referred to in this way. The overall operation to invade occupied northwest Europe was called Overlord, while the assault on the Normandy beaches was codenamed Neptune.

Invasion of the codenames

Planning for Overlord had been active since the Casablanca conference of January 1943, and the operation was given the go-ahead at the Quebec conference in August of that year. Supreme Headquarters Allied Expeditionary Force (SHAEF) was convened in February 1944, under General Dwight Eisenhower, with three British commanders under him in charge of the sea, air, and land arms of the operation, including General Bernard Montgomery. They chose a stretch of the Normandy coastline as their target, and developed exotic supply technology such as floating harbors, codenamed Mulberry, and an undersea cross-Channel oil pipeline codenamed Pluto.

The Atlantic Wall

The Germans knew an amphibious assault was coming and strengthened their Atlantic Wall defenses, but their preparations were fatally hamstrung by disagreements between Field Marshals von Rundstedt and Rommel over the proper strategy. Von Rundstedt wanted to hold back a large force as a mobile reserve able to throw back the Allies after they made their landing, while Rommel wanted to commit the forces to the coastline to stop the Allies getting a foothold in the first place. Hitler adopted an intermediate fudge, and put Rommel in overall command. Rommel had the coastal defenses strengthened and obstacles placed on beaches, and by the end of May 1944 reinforcements brought his strength to two armies, with 25 static coast divisions, 16 infantry and parachute divisions, 10 armored and mechanized divisions, and seven reserve divisions. His air cover, however, was weak, with only 319 aircraft operational on D-Day itself, and his naval forces comprised a mere four destroyers and 39 E-Boats. The lack of air power allowed the Allies to mount a colossal bombing operation; between April 1st and June 5th. Indeed, the historical staff of the Luftwaffe later concluded, "the outstanding factor both before and during the invasion was the overwhelming air superiority of the enemy."

▼ American troops landing at Omaha Beach on D-Day; two-thirds of these men would become casualties in the space of a few hours.

Operation Fortitude

In the event, Rommel was away on leave on the day the invasion was launched. This was just one indicator of the remarkable success of Fortitude: the Allied operation to conceal the intended target region of Overlord, and feed the Germans false information. Fortitude was probably the greatest deception operation in human history, and it worked well enough to convince Hitler that the

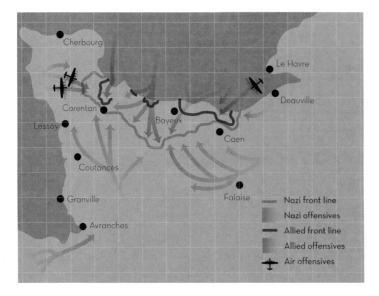

Map showing the amphibious landings, parachute drops, and initial bridgehead secured in the opening days of Operation Fortitude.

Normandy landings were a diversion from the Allies' main target area, the Pas de Calais, with the result that he fatally hesitated to commit his armored reserve to push back the bridgehead.

Assault on Normandy

Just after midnight on June 6th, 23,400 U.S. and British paratroopers landed in Normandy. The 101st U.S. Airborne Division made Sainte-Mère-Église the first village in France to be liberated. At 06:30 the amphibious assault began, with naval assault forces hitting five target beach zones, codenamed (east to west) Sword, Juno, Gold, Omaha, and Utah. Omaha saw the worst fighting, with 2,400 casualties out of 34,000 troops landed, whereas at Utah beach there were only 197 casualties out of 23,000 troops landed. By the time Neptune was officially over, on June 30th, 850,279 men, 148,803 vehicles, and 570,505 tons of supplies had been landed. However, it would take until July 25th for the Allies to break through the German armor containing them in Normandy, and in the first few weeks alone Allied casualties were over 160,000.

250,000

Marchers in the
March on Washington

On August 28th, 1963, around 250,000 people of all races joined in a civil rights demonstration in Washington, D.C. The March on Washington for Jobs and Freedom, sometimes now referred to as the Great March on Washington, was organized partly to lend impetus to a civil rights bill that was at that time making its way through Congress.

One of the main organizers was Martin Luther King, Jr., a Baptist minister and civil rights leader who had shot to national and international prominence in 1955-56 after organizing a bus boycott in Montgomery, Alabama, to protest Rosa Park's arrest for violating racial-segregation laws. King was one of the organizers of the March on Washington, and his electrifying "I have a dream" address has gone down as one of history's greatest speeches. Invoking the Bible and the U.S. Declaration of Independence, King prophesied a future in which, "one day on the red hills of Georgia the sons of former slaves and the sons of former slaveowners will be able to sit down together at the table of brotherhood," going on to tell the crowd, "I have a dream that my four little children will one day live in a nation where they will not be judged by the color of their skin but by the content of their character."

In 1963 King gave 350 speeches and traveled 275,000 miles (442,570 km), winning *Time* magazine's Man of the Year Award, followed by the Nobel Peace Prize in 1964. The legislation that was the target of the March, the landmark Civil Rights Act, passed through Congress in 1964.

▼ Bayard Rustin and Cleveland Robinson, two of the organizers of the March on Washington.

500,000

Volumes in the Library
of Alexandria

The legendary Library of Alexandria in Egypt was said to have contained 500,000 volumes, comprising all the knowledge of the ancient world, before it was destroyed in one of the greatest acts of cultural vandalism in history. In comparison, the next greatest library of antiquity, the Library of Pergamon, traditional rival to Alexandria, was said to contain 200,000 volumes, while there was no library in Rome that had more than 20,000.

Founded by the second of the Ptolemies, using the collection of Aristotle as a nucleus, the Library was said to have really taken off during the reign of the bibliophile Ptolemy III. He supposedly had every arriving ship diligently searched for scrolls to copy, and borrowed the entire collection of Athens, preferring to forfeit his vast deposit rather than give them back. Later it was alleged that Mark Antony transferred the whole of the Pergamon Library to Alexandria as a gift to Cleopatra.

Who killed the Library?

The vast extent of the Alexandrian Library is probably a historical myth, and its story is muddled and often misunderstood. Firstly, there was more than one library in Alexandria. The one generally referred to as *the* Library was the Royal Library, sited in the Temple of the Muses. But there was a "daughter" library, the Serapeum, which probably long outlived its "parent." The fate of these libraries remains a great mystery. Traditionally their destruction was blamed either on Julius Caesar, who set fire to part of Alexandria in 48–47 BCE; or to a fundamentalist Christian mob, incited to destroy pagan temples by the Patriarch Theophilus in 391 CE; or to the Caliph Omar, who, on conquering the city for Islam in 640 CE, is supposed to have decreed that all the scrolls in the Library should be burned, as those that contradicted the Koran were heretical while those that agreed with it were superfluous.

▲ Imaginative reconstruction of the burning of the Library by a fundamentalist mob in 391 CE.

In fact there is little or no evidence that these legends are true. Most likely the various libraries declined and were broken up during the multiple convulsions that afflicted Alexandria throughout the Roman period. The claim that the Library held 500,000 volumes is also probably fanciful. Historian James Hannam has calculated that storing 500,000 scrolls would require 25 miles (40 km) of shelving, necessitating a colossal building of which no trace remains. Evidence from ancient libraries where traces have survived show that the Library of Trajan, the finest in the history of Rome, probably had around 20,000 volumes, while the Library of Pergamon probably had only 30,000. One of the few pieces of evidence about the Alexandrian collection is the *Pinakes*, a detailed index of the Library's contents made by Callimachus, one of the librarians. The Pinakes consisted of about 120 scrolls, which equates to about a million words, suggesting that it cannot have listed extensive information about more than 50,000 volumes.

500,000

Size of annual tax assessment
(sheets of paper)

In the 7th and 8th centuries Tang China was the greatest, most advanced and populous state in the world. Everything about it was superlative. It had the world's largest city, in Chang'an (present day Xi'an), which had over a million inhabitants.

The Tang Dynasty was established by the Sui Dynasty general Li Yuan, the Duke of Tang, who had by 624 imposed order on China after the Sui Dynasty collapsed in 618. Li Yuan became emperor as Gaozu, but was soon ousted by his son Taizong (r. 626–49), who inaugurated a golden age of Chinese culture, military success, and economic development. Among Taizong's achievements were his consolidation of the Sui Dynasty civil service exam system and a massive expansion of the bureaucratic machinery of the state, increasing centralization. By 733 the Tang state employed 17,680 civil servants.

The technological advance of paper was crucial in facilitating this bureaucratic revolution. For instance, the annual tax assessments required over 500,000 sheets of paper, each measuring around 12 by 18 inches (30 x 46 cm), equivalent to an area of 750,000 square feet (~69,500 m²), enough to cover nine soccer pitches. Perhaps the abundance of paper also facilitated poetry, for in this regard also the Tang Dynasty was superlative: nearly 50,000 works by 2,000 Tang poets survive.

▲ Emperor Taizong, aka Li Shimin, generally regarded as one of the greatest of Chinese emperors.

640,000

Men of the Grande Armée
lost by Napoleon in Russia

In December 1810, the Tsar decreed that Russia would no longer maintain alliance with France and adherence to the Continental System, Napoleon's attempt to impose an economic blockade on England. Napoleon planned a campaign to bring the Tsar to heel, summoning troops from every corner of his massive European empire. Men and materiel flooded in from France, Belgium, Holland, Germany, Italy, Prussia, Austria, Denmark, Spain, Portugal, Switzerland, and the Grand Duchy of Warsaw. By 1812 Napoleon had assembled a Grande Armée of staggering size; estimates of its total extent vary from 400,000 to 700,000, alongside 250,000 horses and 2,000 cannon.

A short walk into Russia

The logistics of feeding such a colossal force were extreme, especially because the geography of Russia meant he would rely on a baggage train that included 1,500 wagons and 50,000 draft horses. Napoleon hoped to follow his usual strategy: he would engage the enemy in a decisive battle, destroy its army, and force its ruler to sue for peace. Accordingly, he did not expect to have to travel too far into Russia, but even so he expected his soldiers to bear up. "The first qualification of a soldier is fortitude under fatigue and privation," he once remarked. "Hardship, poverty, and want are the best school for a soldier." His great army would soon be taught the harshest of lessons.

Crossing the Niemen river on June 24th, the men of the Grande Armée were in good spirits and magnificent uniforms. By the time they crossed back over the Niemen on December 14th, there would be as few as 10,000 left, dressed in tatters and close to death from starvation and hypothermia; up to 640,000 men had been lost in less than six months. What had gone so disastrously wrong?

Various ordeals

Initially the Russians frustrated Napoleon through sheer incompetence. Unable to establish a defensive line, they simply fell back, denying Napoleon the decisive action he craved. Finally at Borodino, near Moscow, on September 6th, the Russians were brought to bear in one of the bloodiest battles of all time. The Russians withdrew, leaving Napoleon a Pyrrhic victory that turned to ash in his grasp when he entered Moscow a few days later to find it deserted and set ablaze. The Tsar stubbornly refused to sue for peace and Napoleon's situation worsened with each day he spent in Russia, particularly when winter set in. The retreat back to friendly territory was a hellish nightmare of cold, hunger, and brutal harrying by Cossacks and Russian peasantry.

▼ Napoleon surveys the burning ruins of Moscow, in a painting of 1841 by Albrecht Adam.

One of the most famous infographics in history, by Charles Joseph Minard, graphically depicts the terrible withering of the Grande Armée. It was said to be "the map that made a nation cry," with a thick red line corresponding to the mass of men who entered Russia, while a progressively wasting black line creeps back to the start for the return journey.

1 million

Lies attributed to Marco Polo

Marco Polo's account of his travels in the Far East and adventures at the court of Kublai Khan, written ca. 1299, was popularly known as *Il Milione*—"The Million." This is usually taken to be a reference to widespread skepticism about Polo's astonishing tale, suggesting that his story comprised "a million lies," but it may be that it was actually a reference to his supposed great wealth. Polo was said to have insisted he had played down his adventures, claiming, "I have not told even half of the things that I have seen." The title of the earliest version of the book, written in French, is *Le Divisement dou Monde* ("The Description of the World").

The book was written in jail in Genoa; Marco Polo had been taken prisoner by the Genoese while commanding a Venetian war galley at the Battle of Curzola in 1298. Locked up with him was a romance writer, Rustichello of Pisa, who apparently convinced Polo to let him record the epic tale. Marco Polo claimed, as a teenager, to have traveled with his father and uncle along the Silk Road to Cathay (China), where the emperor Kublai Khan took an interest in him. Polo said that he had served as governor of a city and traveled widely in lands that would not be visited by another European for centuries, before returning home by sea, by way of Southeast Asia and the Indian Ocean, reaching Venice 24 years after leaving. Polo's tale inspired later European explorers and dreamers. Henry the Navigator, the Portuguese prince who sponsored expeditions around Africa to the Indies, was a fan, while Christopher Columbus owned a Latin edition.

1 million

Stone blocks used to construct the Great Enclosure

Great Zimbabwe is the greatest archaeological site in sub-Saharan Africa, preserving remains of what was once the center of the Mwene Mutapa empire of the Shona people, which flourished from around the 12th to 15th centuries CE. The most impressive structure at the site is the Great Enclosure, a huge elliptical space enclosed by a giant wall, 800 feet (244 m) around and up to 33 feet (10 m) high in places. Constructed from two layers of granite blocks, it is perhaps the most extraordinary drystone wall in the world, comprising almost a million blocks.

The Mwene Mutapa empire grew rich from the 12th century thanks to control of trade networks between the African interior, producing ivory, iron, and especially gold, and the Arabic merchants on the East African coast. Goods found at Great Zimbabwe, such as Chinese silk and porcelain, Persian faience, and Indian beads, show the reach of these trade networks. Vast wealth flowed through the hands of the king, or *mambo*, of Mwene Mutapa, and this helped draw a thriving population to Great Zimbabwe.

House of the great women

The purpose of the Great Enclosure remains unclear, but one possible translation of *Imbahuru*, its Shona name, is "house of the great woman." This fed into the racist assumptions of the first European visitors to Great Zimbabwe, who developed far-fetched theories about Great Zimbabwe as the lost city of Ophir, home of the Biblical Queen of Sheba. This and similar theories became part of the racist ideology of the Rhodesian colony.

1 million

People died in the Great Famine of Ireland

The Great Famine of 1845-49 devastated the population of Ireland, with around a million people dying of disease or starvation, and another million forced to emigrate. The population crashed from around 8 million to 6 million, and the steady flow of emigration continued for another century. Ireland's population has never recovered to its pre-Famine levels.

Potato blight

The Great Famine is also popularly known as the Potato Famine, because it resulted from the outbreak of potato blight (caused by the fungus *Phytophthora infestans*), which caused the potato crop to fail. By 1845 potato was the most important crop in Ireland. Over 2 million acres (809,000 hectares) of land were growing potatoes, and over 3 million people depended entirely on them for sustenance. Up to 15 lb (7 kg) of potatoes were eaten daily per person, sometimes at three meals a day. Potatoes were also the main feedstock for pigs, which themselves formed another mainstay for Irish farmers as a source of protein and income.

The blight arrived in September 1845; potatoes rotted in the ground and the crop failed. The blight struck again in 1846, and although it lifted in 1847, not enough seed potatoes had been planted to give a decent crop, and then the disease returned in 1848 and '49. Deprived of the potato's rich supply of vitamin C, the affected population were afflicted with scurvy, marasmus, and

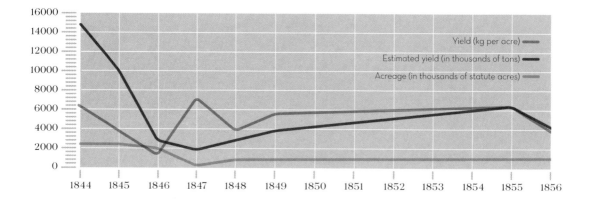

kwashiorkor. Vitamin A deficiencies caused widespread
xerophthalmia, blinding many workhouse children. As the starving
converged on cities and crammed into workhouses, typhus and
other crowd diseases struck. Scenes of Biblical horror played out,
with mass graves, hunger marches, and unburied corpses.

▲ Graph showing the
catastrophic decline in
the size of the potato crop
in Ireland between 1844
and 1845, and how the
acreage under potatoes
was halved thanks to the
subsequent depopulation.

Paying for poverty

Ireland was part of Great Britain, at this time the richest nation
on Earth, yet the British government's response was hopelessly
inadequate. In the late spring of 1847, finally waking up to the
magnitude of the disaster, the government opened soup kitchens,
but these were soon shut down, with new laws introduced to make
"Irish property pay for Irish poverty." This failed to halt the ravages
of the famine, but did provoke a massive wave of evictions that
saw hundreds of thousands turned off the land. Many landlords
paid for their tenants to emigrate to Britain and America.

One consequence of the famine was to set Irish public opinion
irredeemably against British rule. The uncaring English, touting
their callous creed of *laissez-faire*, were blamed for the crisis;
hence the famous words of nationalist and writer John Mitchel:
"The Almighty sent the potato blight, but the English created the
famine." After the famine abated, Irish living standards and real
wages did increase, but emigration continued to drain the
population, and the psychic scars of the Great Famine linger on.

6 million

Jewish victims of the Holocaust

The Holocaust is one name given to the systematic slaughter of European Jewry by the Nazis, which they called the Final Solution (*Endlösung*). Technically the Final Solution was implemented from late 1941, but Jewish organizations date the start of the Holocaust to 1933, when Hitler came to power in Germany. The Nazis viewed the Jews as an alien, "polluting" strain in the German population, and to solve what they called the *Judenfrage* (Jewish Question), they proposed a series of "solutions," which evolved as Nazi Germany absorbed more territory and more Jews came under their control.

The emigration solution

In 1933 there were half a million Jews in Germany, although the 1935 Nuremberg Laws, defining Jewishness as having had one Jewish grandparent, probably boosted this number. The first solution was to move Jews out of the countryside, villages, and small towns, and into larger towns and cities. The second solution was emigration, which was initially the Nazis' preferred option. By 1938 more than half of German Jews had emigrated, mostly to America, Argentina, Britain, and Palestine, but also to France, Poland, and other parts of Europe. Concentration camps were set up in Germany around this time, but they were primarily for political prisoners. Another 250,000 Jews came under Nazi control after the annexation of Austria and parts of

Czechoslovakia, in 1938, but even after the attacks of *Kristallnacht* (see page 93), emigration remained the primary solution envisaged by the regime. Around this time, however, many destination states began to restrict Jewish immigration. The possibilities for emigration further diminished after the German invasion of Poland in September 1939. The coming of war, a British naval blockade, and the restriction of civilian transport throughout German territory, all conspired to make emigration impractical, even as the number of Jews under Nazi control increased by another 1.5 million.

In Poland a third solution developed, of concentrating Jews into a few ghettos. Deliberately overcrowded and undersupplied, these ghettos would both provide a source of forced labor and effect a slow extermination of the Jewish populace. By April 1941 half a million Jews were confined in the Warsaw Ghetto, and by June they were dying of starvation and illness at the rate of 2,000 a month. German conquests in 1940–41 brought under their control the Jewish populations of Norway (1,400), Denmark (5,600), France (283,000), the Netherlands (126,000), Luxembourg (1,700), Belgium (64,000), and Greece (77,000).

The "Final Solution"

A horrific fourth solution was implemented with the June 1941 invasion of the Soviet Union. Following behind the advancing troops came *Einsatzgruppen*, special killing squads, tasked with immediate elimination of local Jewish populations. Assisted by local security forces and paramilitaries, and by Romanian forces, around a million Jews would be murdered by a combination of mass shootings, burnings, beatings, and gassing. Meanwhile preparations were being made for a fifth and final solution: the mass deportation of Jews to remote camps, where they would be gassed, either in special vans or in gas chambers disguised as shower rooms.

The "Final Solution" was implemented at four death camps—Chełmno, Sobibór, Treblinka, and Bełzec—from December 1941, while a fifth camp, Birkenau, attached to an existing concentration

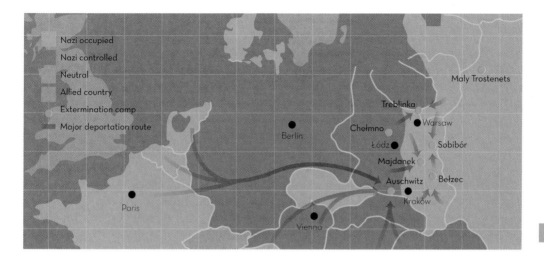

Nazi occupied
Nazi controlled
Neutral
Allied country
Extermination camp
Major deportation route

Maly Trostenets

Treblinka

Berlin

Chełmno

Warsaw

Łódź

Sobibór

Majdanek

Auschwitz

Bełżec

Paris

Kraków

Vienna

camp at Auschwitz, was opened in March 1942. On the pretext of "resettlement," trains brought Jews from all over Europe to German-occupied Poland. The passengers were killed almost immediately on arrival, except at Birkenau where up to half of them would be sent to do forced labor, although most of these would also die. Over 2.5 million Jews were sent to Birkenau, and all but 250,000 of them were murdered there.

From September 1944 the approach of Soviet forces led to the evacuation of Auschwitz-Birkenau. Many of the surviving inmates perished in the subsequent death marches, and those that survived were mostly worked to death in slave labor camps, or distributed to existing concentration camps for political prisoners and criminals, such as Bergen-Belsen and Dachau, where they were tortured and starved. It was in camps such as these that British and American forces, and through them the wider world, first fully encountered the horror of the Final Solution.

Some 6 million Jews, including 1.5 million children, died in the Holocaust, which wiped out one-third of world Jewry and two-thirds of European Jewry. Just 300,000 Jews survived the camps and death marches, and around 10,000 Jewish communities, integral parts of the fabric of Europe for over 1000 years, were destroyed.

▲ Map showing the routes and destinations of Jews deported from around Nazi-controlled Europe during the Final Solution.

12.5 million

Africans shipped to
the New World

The slave trade across the Atlantic was the largest long-distance forced movement of people in history. Between 1525 and 1867, according to the leading authority, the Trans-Atlantic Slave Trade Database, 12.5 million Africans were shipped across the Atlantic, although only 10.7 million survived the Middle Passage. The vast majority went to South America and the Caribbean; only around 450,000 ended up in North America. Brazil, on the other hand, received 4.86 million African slaves.

▼ A slave ship making the Middle Passage ca. 1780; the nature of her cargo is given away by the small ventilation ports in her lower hull.

A gap in the market

The main driver for the slave trade was the need for labor in the New World. Thanks in part to the deadly epidemics they introduced, European colonists had achieved total domination of the New World, and were in a position to exploit it for tropical crops—mainly sugar, but also tobacco, and later cotton—and precious metals, but for this they needed a massive labor force. Those same epidemics, however, had almost completely wiped out the indigenous inhabitants. European immigrants were too few and too unwilling to do the arduous labor involved. Slavery had long since disappeared from northwest Europe, but in the 16th-century European worldview Africans remained eligible for slavery, while in Africa itself there was no overarching sense of pan-African identity to prevent Africans from one tribe or kingdom from selling into slavery those of other, distant groups.

Accordingly a colossal slave trade filled the gap in the market left by European colonists. Up to 1820, for every European who crossed the Atlantic to the New World, four Africans made the journey. Over $^2/_3$ of the slaves went to sugar plantations. Atlantic ocean currents dictated from which parts of Africa slaves would be transported to which parts of the Americas. The clockwise currents in the northern Atlantic meant that most of the slaves who went to North America and the Caribbean were carried by English slavers, and taken from West Africa (the Bights of Biafra and Benin and the Gold Coast), though some also came from Angola. South of the Equator, the counterclockwise currents powered an almost exclusively Portuguese-Brazilian slave trade, carrying slaves mostly from Angola, along with some from southeastern Africa and the Bight of Benin.

The Middle Passage

The transatlantic journey, known as the Middle Passage, was horrific for slaves. Naked and packed close together, slaves were chained below decks for journeys that took, on average, two months. Around a quarter of the slaves on each ship were children. The mortality rate for slaves making the Middle Passage was around 14 percent.

The abolitionist movement in Europe and America eventually made the slave trade illegal, and the British negotiated a series of treaties allowing their navy to stop and search ships of all nations. However, it was not until the Cubans and Brazilians took action in the 1840s and '50s that the trade really declined.

▲ Unfortunate men, women, and children being driven into slavery.

16,410,030

Shares sold on Black Tuesday

The Wall Street Crash of 1929 saw records tumble. A massive bubble of stock speculation had taken the value of shares on the New York Stock Exchange (NYSE) to extraordinary heights. Its stock prices doubled in the 1920s. In 1927, the value of securities increased by over 37 percent, and in 1928 by over 43 percent. Speculation became a national pastime; brokerages opened offices at hotels and a golf championship. Joseph Kennedy, patriarch of the Kennedy clan, later claimed that he sold out in 1928 after hearing a shoeshine boy giving out stock tips. On September 3rd, 1929, the Dow Jones Industrial Average peaked at 381.17—it would not reach that level again for nearly 25 years. Two days later came the first in a series of ever-greater drops.

On Black Tuesday, October 29th, 1929, 3 million shares were sold in the first 30 minutes of trading on the NYSE. By the end of the day, 16,410,030 shares had been sold. In October 1929 the NYSE saw $50 billion wiped off stocks, more than the U.S. had spent on World War I. Between September 1929 and 1932, the value of stocks on the NYSE dropped from $90 billion to $16 billion, and the value of the Dow Jones fell by 89 percent.

Although the Wall Street Crash did not cause the Great Depression that followed, it contributed. The American economy did not recover until World War II. During the Great Depression the real gross national product (GNP) fell by 30 percent, prices dropped by 23 percent, and unemployment was at 24 percent or higher.

30 million

English national debt in 1720 (£)

In 1720 the English national debt of £30 million was underwritten by the South Sea Company, a trading monopoly with corrupt links to the establishment. This was part of a deal in which the company loaned the government £7 million up front, to finance the ongoing war with France, in return for passage through Parliament of the South Sea Bill, which bestowed upon the company a monopoly of trade with South America. The national debt was underwritten by the company on the promise of 5 percent annual interest until 1727 and 4 percent thereafter.

This amazingly good deal for the South Sea Company resulted in the South Sea Bubble, one of the greatest speculative bubbles of all time. Shares in the company immediately rocketed in value, from £128 in January 1720 to £1,000 in August. This touched off a speculative frenzy in which the demand for investments was so intense that increasingly ludicrous schemes found instant backing.

The Bubble collapsed in August, ruining speculators rich and poor, and exposed vast impropriety: 462 members of the House of Commons and 112 Peers held shares in the South Sea Company, along with intimate associates of King George I himself.

▼ During the Bubble an enterprise "For carrying-on an undertaking of great advantage but no-one to know what it is" somehow secured £2,000 in investment.

78 million

Market capitalization of Dutch East India Company (guilders)

In 1637 the market capitalization of the Dutch East India Company was 78 million Dutch guilders, equivalent to $7.4 trillion in 2012 U.S. dollars, making it history's most valuable company.

The Dutch East India Company, known in Holland as the *Verenigde Oostindische Compagnie* (VOC), was created in 1602 with the world's first IPO. It was formed to finance the increasingly expensive trips Dutch merchants were undertaking to the Far East. In the wake of their war with the Spanish, the Dutch provinces had achieved naval superiority and greatly widened the reach of their trading empire, and the VOC fitted out ships for long and dangerous journeys to the East Indies where it worked to monopolize the spice trade. By the end of the 17th century it had a monopoly on nutmeg, mace, and cloves and controlled most of the market in pepper, as well as lucrative trading in tea, coffee, and opium. Eventually it moved into trading textiles and fabrics. Over two centuries the VOC built almost 1,500 ships that carried over a million people. In 1669, for instance, it had 150 trading vessels, 40 warships, and 10,000 soldiers in its service.

The voyages of the VOC could bring profits of 10,000 percent, but it reached its highest capitalization in the course of the tulipmania bubble. Even after that bubble subsided, the VOC proved itself to be a worthy investment, paying out an 18 percent annual dividend for many years, although it eventually became mired in corruption and debt, and after repeated bailouts was wound up by the Dutch government in 1798.

350 million

People watching the
coronation of Elizabeth II

The Coronation of Elizabeth II on June 2nd, 1953, was one of the great media events of the age. In Britain, the fact that it would be televised helped sustain a boom in television ownership, while film of the event shipped around the world and shown on television and as newsreel helped make the Queen the most famous woman in the world, and the most photographed of all time.

With the vigorous backing of Prime Minister Winston Churchill, the state's preparations for the Coronation were lavish, and it was seen as a chance to break free of postwar austerity. For instance, Churchill ordered that rationing of candy for children would end the day before.

The Coronation Day itself was rainy and dull but huge crowds turned out to watch the procession, and far larger ones would watch television and film footage of the event. The ceremony was broadcast live on radio and TV around the world in 44 different languages, and a quarter of the world's population took June 2nd off in celebration. Even as the Queen and a procession of 16,000 people made their way back from Westminster Abbey to Buckingham Palace after the ceremony, film of the coronation service was on an airplane to Canada, where it would be broadcast within four hours of the end of the ceremony. In the UK the viewing audience for the television broadcast of the ceremony was 27 million (half the population), while the eventual global audience for footage of the Coronation was 350 million.

▲ Coronation portrait of the Queen and Prince Philip, the Duke of Edinburgh.

200 billion

Cost of World War I (U.S.$)

World War I was fought at fantastic cost in treasure as well as blood. The total amount spent by all the combatant nations was more than $200 billion. Where did this money come from? If governments did not have enough money they had to borrow it, and the Allies had the advantage of being able to turn to the United States. In 1916 the U.S. Federal Reserve noted, "the United States is fast becoming the banker of foreign countries in all parts of the world." Around 1,500 U.S. banks conducted bond sales and loan arrangements in World War I, with J. P. Morgan alone leading the underwriting of $1.5 billion in loans to the British and French. The U.S. government loaned its Allies almost $12 billion during World War I. By 1918, Britain would owe the United States over £800 million, and France £600 million (at a time when the exchange rate was around $2.5 to £1). At the same time the U.S. government had to borrow to finance its own war effort, raising over $18 billion through a program of Liberty Loans, and spending about $36 billion on the war as a whole.

The net result at the end of the war was vast increases in national debts. British National Debt in 1914 was £650 million; by 1918 it was £2,000 million and by 1923, £6,657 million. U.S. National Debt increased even more sharply, from $1 billion in 1914 to $25 billion by 1919. Britain is still paying interest on bonds issued to cover World War I debt. In 1965, 1 percent of British income tax revenue was being used to repay American loans from World War I.

400 billion

Net worth of Mansa Musa, king of Mali (U.S.$)

Mansa Musa ruled the empire of Mali from 1312 to 1337, securing and extending its borders until it stretched across a vast swathe of Africa, from the Middle Niger, through Timbuktu and Gao, north into the Sahara and east into Hausaland and even as far as Western Sudan. He was believed to control half of the world's supply of salt and gold, and his empire stood at the crossroads between great networks of trade.

Thanks to the records of contemporary Islamic historians such as al-'Umari and Ibn Battuta, Mansa Musa has become famous for the extraordinary impact of his arrival in Cairo during his pilgrimage to Mecca in 1324. Accompanied by 500 personal servants, 60,000 porters, and 10,000 soldiers, he also brought along 20 tons of gold. One witness said that his entourage included porters carrying "80 packages of gold dust, each weighing three *kintars* (8½ lb, or 3.8 kg)... and 500 slaves, each carrying a golden staff weighing over 500 *mithkal* (about 6½ lb, or 3 kg)."

The arrival of so much gold caused rampant inflation and the devaluation of Egyptian currency. According to the website Celebrity Net Worth, Mansa Musa's fortune equated to $400 billion at 2013 gold prices, making him the richest person who ever lived.

▼ Detail from the Catalan Atlas of 1375, showing Mansa Musa displaying some of his vast wealth in gold.

Further reading

Books

Beevor, A. *D-Day: The Battle for Normandy* London, 2009

Bowersock, G., P. Brown, and O. Grabar (Eds.) *Late Antiquity: A Guide to the Postclassical World* Cambridge, MA: Harvard University Pres, 1999

Calvocoressi, P. *World Politics Since 1945* London: Routledge, 2009

Carlisle, R. *Encyclopedia of Intelligence & Counterintelligence* London: Routledge, 2005

Chaffee, John *The Thorny Gates of Learning in Sung China: A Social History of Examinations* Albany: State University of New York Press, 1995

Cull, N., D. Culbert, and D. Welch *Propaganda and Mass Persuasion: A Historical Encyclopedia, 1500 to the Present* Santa Barbara, CA: ABC-CLIO, 2003

Davies, Martin *The Gutenberg Bible* London: British Library, ca. 1996

Diamond, Jared *Collapse* London: Allen Lane, 2005

Dunn, Richard S. *The Age of Religious Wars: 1559-1715* 2nd ed. New York: Norton, 1979

Fagan, Brian M. (Ed.) *The Oxford Companion to Archaeology* Oxford University Press, 1996

Foner, E., and J. Garraty (Eds.) *The Reader's Companion to American History* Boston, MA: Houghton Mifflin, 2014

Furay, Conal, and Michael J. Salevouris *The Methods and Skills of History* 4th edn. John Wiley & Sons, 2015

Herzog, Chaim *The Arab-Israeli Wars: War and Peace in the Middle East* Barnsley: Frontline Books, 2010

Israel, Jonathan *The Dutch Republic* Oxford: Clarendon Press, 1995

Jacobs, Els M. *In Pursuit of Pepper and Tea: The Story of the Dutch East India Company* Amsterdam: Walburg Pers, 1991

Kaufman, W., and H. Macpherson (Eds.) *Britain and the Americas: Culture, Politics, and History* Santa Barbara, CA: ABC-CLIO, 2005

Knight, P. (Ed.) *Conspiracy Theories in American History* Santa Barbara, CA: ABC-CLIO, 2003

Krieger, Joel (Ed.) *Oxford Companion to Politics of the World* [2nd edn.] Oxford University Press, 2001

Kurtz, L. (Ed.) *Encyclopedia of Violence, Peace and Conflict* Oxford: Elsevier Science & Technology, 2008

Levathes, Louise *When China Ruled the Seas: The Treasure Fleet of the Dragon Throne, 1405-1433* Oxford University Press, 1994

Levy, Joel *History's Worst Battles* London: New Burlington Books, 2012

Levy, Joel *Lost Cities* London: New Holland, 2008

Levy, Joel *Lost Histories* London: Vision, 2006

Mackenzie, J. (Ed.) *Cassell's Peoples, Nations and Cultures* London: Cassell, 2005

Markham, J. *A Financial History of the United States* London: Routledge, 2002

McGinn, Bernard *Encyclopedia of Apocalypticism, vol. 2* London: Continuum, 1998

Motyl, A. (Ed.) *Encyclopedia of nationalism: Leaders, movements, and concepts* Oxford, United Kingdom: Elsevier Science & Technology, 2001

Nolan, C. Greenwood *Encyclopedia of International Relations* Santa Barbara, CA: ABC-CLIO, 2002

1

Northrup, C. Clark (Ed.) *Encyclopedia of World Trade: From Ancient Times to the Present* London: Routledge, 2013

Parker, Geoffrey *The Thirty Years' War* London: Routledge & Kegan Paul, 1984

Parry, Dan *Moonshot: The Inside Story of Mankind's Greatest Adventure* London: Ebury Press, 2009

Phillips, J. *Holy Warriors: A Modern History of the Crusades* London: Bodley Head, 2009

Pocock, Tom *Battle for Empire: The Very First World War, 1756-63* London: M. O'Mara, 1998

Wade, Rex A. *The Russian Revolution, 1917* New York: Cambridge University Press, 2005

Waldron, Arthur *The Great Wall of China: From History to Myth* Cambridge: Cambridge University Press, 1990

Whyte, I. *A Dictionary of Environmental History* London: I. B. Tauris, 2013

Wills, Garry *Lincoln at Gettysburg: The Words that Remade America* New York: Simon & Schuster, 1992

Wright, Lawrence *The Looming Tower: Al-Qaeda and the Road to 9/11* New York, NY: Vintage, 2007

Ziegler, Philip *The Black Death* London: Collins, 1969

Useful websites

Council for British Archaeology
http://new.archaeologyuk.org/

Encyclopaedia Romana http://penelope.uchicago.edu/~grout/encyclopaedia_romana/index.html

Eyewitness to History www.eyewitnesstohistory.com

History Net www.historynet.com

MacTutor History of Mathematics archive
www-history.mcs.st-and.ac.uk

NASA History Program http://history.nasa.gov/

Smithsonian Magazine www.smithsonianmag.com

The Domesday Book online www.domesdaybook.co.uk

The Great War www.greatwar.co.uk

The Magna Carta Project
http://magnacarta.cmp.uea.ac.uk

The Trans-Atlantic Slave Trade Database
www.slavevoyages.org

Tolpuddle Martyrs Museum
www.tolpuddlemartyrs.org.uk

Index

Picture credits